PAINTING ○ COLOR ○ HISTORY

COLLECTION PLANNED AND DIRECTED BY
ALBERT SKIRA

AMERICAN PAINTING

From Its Beginnings to the Armory Show

INTRODUCTION BY

JOHN WALKER

TEXT BY

JULES DAVID PROWN

SKIRA

GENERAL EDITOR OF THIS VOLUME: ALEXIS GREGORY

*

Distributed in the United States by
THE WORLD PUBLISHING COMPANY
2231 West 110th Street, Cleveland, Ohio 44102

*

PRINTED IN SWITZERLAND

Contents

List of Color Plates

Introduction

*T*he history of American painting falls conveniently into triads. There were three main movements: Realist, Romantic, and Primitive art. There were three outstanding colonial painters: West, Copley, and Stuart. No artist measured up to them until the second half of the nineteenth century, when America produced three more masters of the first rank who worked in Europe: Mary Cassatt, Whistler, and Sargent. That same generation brought forth three artists equally distinguished who remained at home: Eakins, Homer, and Ryder. The text of this book brilliantly proves that these nine painters make the American School illustrious by any standards.

Though born in a colonial or a provincial society the first three were among the most advanced artists of their time. West, Jules Prown shows, was a prophet of David and neoclassicism, and both West and Copley were precursors of Géricault and Delacroix. To these I might add Stuart who in theory and to some degree in practice anticipated the Impressionists.

The expatriates at the end of the nineteenth century were equally inventive. Mary Cassatt, working with the Impressionists, reintroduced the mother and child theme and imbued this subject with a dignity not seen since the Madonnas of the Renaissance. Whistler single handed started a movement in Europe and America, Aestheticism, and in Jules Prown's words helped "to establish the theoretical basis for abstract art." Sargent set the standards for fashionable, cosmopolitan portraiture, creating a style which found imitators everywhere.

Though the three masters who remained in this country, Eakins, Homer, and Ryder, had fewer followers, they were in some ways more original. The realism of Eakins was the most intellectual, the most scientific, the most uncompromising among painters of his generation. Homer's studies of hunting and fishing are the best descriptions in art of the pleasures, dangers, even tragedies of men who live out of doors, the various aspects of their contest with nature for pleasure or for existence; just as his studies of waves as they beat relentlessly on the shore or as they gently swell, muffled *in fog, show uniquely both the power and the loneliness of the sea. Ryder, too, in his own way reaches a limit of art. His dream-shrouded world finds no parallel in American painting and few in European art. His style is as original and idiomatic as the poetry of Edgar Allan Poe.*

Henry James was fond of pointing out that "the best things come, as a general thing, from the talents that are members of a group; every man works better when he has companions working in the same line, and yielding the stimulus of suggestion, comparison, emulation." This was not the good fortune of those nineteenth-century American painters who remained in this country. The lives of Homer, Eakins, and Ryder reveal loneliness, isolation, and a failure to communicate with their contemporaries, whether artists or patrons. Nevertheless, in a period of artistic decline, which marked the nineteenth century except in France, solitude may prove a vaccine against the virus of bad taste. Thus the solitary artist may work more healthily when quarantined from his fellows. Partly for this reason it can be asserted, I believe, that from 1860 to 1900 America produced more distinguished painting than any other Western country excepting only France.

But there were factors other than solitude which affected American artists. Their styles were determined by problems uniquely American. There was, for instance, the geographical separation of the New World from Europe. This had an important result especially for young artists. Traditionally painters during their apprenticeship have seen nature through the eyes of their instructors, or if self-taught, through masterpieces available to them in private collections or public museums. Neither the masters nor the models were to be found in America. Even as late as the second half of the nineteenth century Mary Cassatt summed up the situation when she said to an interviewer, "When I was young. . . our museums had no great paintings for the student to study." Thus among American artists there was always a European complex—a longing first for London, and later for Paris or Munich.

Owing to the lack of masters and masterpieces and to the predominantly rural nature of eighteenth- and nineteenth-century America, an exceptional number of American painters were itinerant, self-taught, and unaffected as were European artists by metropolitan fashions. These "primitives" were modest craftsmen, devoid of all pretentiousness. They executed their commissions as skillfully as they could, retaining always an innocence of vision and a strong sense of decoration. They were as far from the bohemian geniuses of the last century we associate with the Left Bank in Paris as they were from the fastidious aesthetes we think of in Chelsea. In this respect they were closer to the artisans of the early Renaissance or those of the late Middle Ages. Perhaps because their work lies outside the mainstream of art, just as they themselves do not fit into our romantic idea of the painter, they have not until now been adequately appreciated.

Apart from the lack of an artistic tradition the American painter was affected in other ways by the New World. He was confronted, for example, by a terrain as unexplored artistically as it was geographically. When he left the Eastern seaboard he was overwhelmed by the vastness of nature. Making a virtue of necessity, he praised the sublimity of this primeval wilderness. But even a genius as great as Turner was unable to express satisfactorily the grandeur of the Alps; what hope was there for the American landscapist to render the stupendous splendor of the Rockies? Nevertheless, he tried repeatedly, and his failures are not without their own magnificence.

In America, light too is less paintable than in Europe. Though the North American continent is so vast that generalization is difficult, still it is apparent that nature has not afforded artists in the New World the equivalent of the broken, dappled sunlight of England and the Low Countries, or the caressing, soft bluish light of France, or the tangible gold of sunset in Italy. Instead, light in America tends to be strong, hard, and sharply brilliant. It brings out local color and exaggerates value contrasts. Perhaps for this reason America has never produced distinguished colorists until the advent of the Abstract Expressionists, who were totally indifferent to natural illumination.

Thus lack of models, lack of a humanized scenery, lack of a painterly light were disadvantages. But there was, on the other hand, the excitement of a new society. Painters were inspired by the spirit which caused Whitman to write in his preface to Leaves of Grass, "The United States themselves are essentially the greatest poem. In the history of the earth hitherto the largest and most stirring appear tame and orderly to their ampler largeness and stir. Here at last is something in the doings of man that corresponds with the broadcast doings of the day and night." Such boasting may now seem to us unattractive, perhaps because we realize how far a hundred years has taken us from Whitman's dream. Nevertheless, it describes the nineteenth-century atmosphere in which American painters thrived.

The dangers facing artists in this country were chauvinism and parochialism. These appear to some degree in the so-called "Ashcan school," which followed the generation of Eakins and Homer. To quote Jules Prown, "Their art dealt with real life and real people. It was democratic art depicting not the aristocratic classes who populated the paintings of the 'genteel tradition' but the lower middle classes, the great mass of the American populace." They believed with Whitman that "the genius of the United States is . . . always most in the common people."

In the 1930's Barbara Rose shows how this populist strain in American painting was encouraged by the Roosevelt WPA programs, but it eventually dwindled into Regionalism and Social Realism. The seeds of its destruction had been sown much earlier by the Armory Exhibition of 1913 where for the first time American artists saw the new movements taking place in Europe. The roots of abstraction were planted. During the First World War and the Great Depression the more progressive painters gradually assimilated these new ideas. During the Second World War whatever was parochial, whatever was provincial, vanished from American art; and at the same time American artists lost a certain innocence, a certain ingenuousness. Ended were those *misjudgments in taste, such as Eakins' admiration for Gérôme, or that insecurity before the Old Masters, which may explain Homer's wish to ignore them, or the lack of a studio tradition, which made Ryder such a weak craftsman. The gain in knowledge meant not only that innocence was lost but that something of more significance disappeared: an unselfconscious integrity, exemplified by Homer's and Eakins' refusal to compromise, by their plodding search for reality, or by Ryder's indifference to popular taste, by his detachment from all that was extraneous to his private vision. In the nineteenth century a blunt honesty was a major characteristic of the native American style, as distinct from the sophistication of the American expatriates. It was a style brusque, awkward, naive at times; but there was on the one hand a heartfelt struggle for actuality, and on the other a brooding, Romantic vision.*

In our day American painting has become more subtle, more inventive, more cosmopolitan. With the emergence of Abstract Expressionism the torch of artistic revolution has burnt in New York and not in Paris. Pollock, de Kooning, and Motherwell led the "action" painters of the 1940's; they were followed by the "color field" painters: Still, Newman, Rothko, and Reinhardt. These in turn were succeeded by the hard-edge or post-painterly abstractionists: Frankenthaler, Noland, Olitski, Stella, Kelly, and others. There has also been a return to figurative painting in the pop-art movement, a combination of the comic strip and Madison Avenue advertising.

When one considers this extraordinary development of the School of New York it can be argued convincingly that leadership in painting has passed to this continent. The question remains, and only time will tell, whether these new American leaders are going in directions as significant as did their more innocent forebears.

JOHN WALKER

AMERICAN PAINTING

From Its Beginnings to the Armory Show

Anonymous. Mrs. Elizabeth Freake and Daughter Mary, about 1674. (42½×36¾″)
Owned by the Worcester Art Museum, Worcester, Massachusetts. Gift of Mr. and Mrs. Albert W. Rice.

The Colonial Period

THE most obvious fact about early American painting is that there was so little of it. When European colonists began to establish permanent settlements on the eastern flank of North America, they had other things on their minds than the painting of pictures. Faced with a pressing necessity to satisfy their primary life needs—food, shelter, clothing—they adopted a way of life and a view of the world that was necessarily pragmatic. For them the arts seemed dangerously irrelevant, a distraction from the serious tasks at hand. As an anonymous writer in Boston put it: "The Plow-man that raiseth Grain is more serviceable to Mankind, than the Painter who draws only to please the eye. The hungry man would count fine Pictures, but a mean entertainment. The Carpenter who builds a good House to defend us from the Wind and Weather, is more serviceable than the curious Carver, who employs his Art to please his fancy. This condemns not Painting, or Carving, but only shows, that what's more substantially serviceable to Mankind, is much preferable to what is less necessary." That pragmatic attitude has characterized American culture from its inception to the present day, and has profoundly affected the trajectory of American art.

The earliest surviving American colonial painting, a portrait of *Elizabeth Eggington* (Wadsworth Atheneum, Hartford, Connecticut), inscribed with the date 1664, was painted long after the establishment of the first permanent English settlements at Jamestown in Virginia (1607) and Plymouth in Massachusetts (1620). Although it may be said that American art began with *Elizabeth Eggington*, it must at the same time be pointed out that a considerable body of pre-colonial, non-colonial and neighboring-colonial art might make the same claim. For example, early expeditions of exploration before the period of settlement often carried artists among their complement to record the physical facts of America. Curious Europeans wanted to see pictures of the New World and its inhabitants. Artists also participated in several of the abortive sixteenth century attempts at settlement in North America; notably Jacque Le Moyne de Morgues (d. 1588) who arrived in 1564 with a Huguenot settlement in Florida and fortuitously escaped when that settlement was wiped out by the Spanish the following year, and John White (active 1584-1593) who joined Sir Walter Raleigh's ill-fated venture at Roanoke in Virginia in 1585. However the pictures made by explorer-artists, fascinating as they are, were in fact the work of Europeans who happened only by circumstance to be working briefly in America. Their art belongs to the New World only in its subject matter, and even the *reportage* was affected by European modes of seeing. Sixteenth century American Indians often are given distinctly Mannerist proportions.

Also antedating *Elizabeth Eggington* is a corpus of provincial art, much of it religious, limited in quality as well as quantity, produced in the Spanish colonial areas of Florida, Louisiana and the American Southwest within the borders of the present continental United States. However this peripheral art properly belongs to the history of Central and South American painting. Similarly the French colonial art of Detroit and the Mississippi River Valley fits in more appropriately with the history of Canadian art. The artistic production of the Dutch in New York and the Swedish along the lower Delaware in colonies soon overrun by the British was, unfortunately, limited and minor.

It is more difficult to justify not beginning our study with the art of the American Indian, the art of the peoples resident here before the Europeans came. Yet this elimination is in fact consistent with what actually happened in the development of American art and American civilization. Whereas Spanish colonies in Central and South America absorbed local cultures, converting the natives to Catholicism in the process, the English settlers in North America disdained the Indian, annihilated his civilization whenever it got in the way, and absorbed virtually nothing from the culture of the American Indian.

Thus the tentative and halting beginnings of what eventually broadened into the mainstream of American painting are found in those pictures painted during the seventeenth century in the English colonies strung along the Atlantic seaboard from Maine to Georgia, the colonies that eventually banded together to form the United States of America. Extraordinarily little is known about painting in America in the seventeenth century; almost no documentation exists. The primary evidence is provided by perhaps half a hundred surviving paintings, all of them portraits. Artists are for the most part unidentified, although pictures have been tentatively assigned to discrete hands on the basis of style and sitter groups. It is obvious, if only from the paucity of surviving pictures, that these were not full-time artists, but perhaps unspecialized painters who wielded their brushes on walls and wagons, signs and portraits alike, as opportunities arose. The compositions used in the portraits are few and mannered. Children are shown at full-length, standing on checkered black-and-white tile floors, clutching a glove, fan, bird, cane, flower or piece of fruit. Men are half or three-quarters length; clergymen clutching a Bible and laymen toying with gloves. Women are seated, often holding a child in their laps. Heads are shifted slightly to left or right, the eyes staring forward. Both hands are invariably shown.

The portrait of *Elizabeth Eggington* presaged a sudden and still unexplained flurry of artistic activity in Boston about 1670. Undoubtedly a major factor must have been the arrival of one or more able artists, the best of whom, identified today only as the Freake limner, painted what is perhaps the most beautiful of all seventeenth century American paintings, *Mrs. Elizabeth Freake and Daughter Mary*. Mrs. Freake sits on a Cromwellian sidechair upholstered with turkeywork, her daughter standing on her lap. A curtain is pulled back to the upper left. The subjects in most of the earliest portraits were endowed with a similar appearance by the limners—small faces, almond-shaped eyes, high foreheads, wide cheekbones. Here the faces of mother and child are drawn with unusual sensitivity by the artist, but even so, they are devoid of personality and no more important than the stuffs that surround them, the dresses, petticoats, lace, hoods, ribbons and jewelry. The palette of black, white, yellow, green, red, and brown is limited but strong. Indeed color is a primary pictorial element. The traditional view of seventeenth century Americans as dour, ascetic, puritanical, and unresponsive to the sensuous pleasures of life is contradicted by the evidence before our eyes of people who enjoyed bright colors, finery and material comfort.

Although as our eye moves from the bright red embroidered petticoat in the lower left through the child to Mrs. Freake, the chair, and the background, we comprehend a recession in space, no real illusion of space is in fact presented. The picture is constructed of precisely outlined areas of strong local color juxtaposed to form a two-dimensional pattern in relief against the dark background. The picture surface is all-important, strongly affirmed by areas of intense color and embroidered with linear detail. The planar emphasis and bright color, normal in unsophisticated or primitive art, would not be unexpected in the work of anonymous limners who painted signs as well as portraits. Yet the quality of the drawing suggests that the style may reflect conscious esthetic selection fully as much as, or even more than, insufficiency of technique.

The brilliant color, the determined linearity and the insistent emphasis of the picture surface recalls both Elizabethan portraiture, as in the miniatures of Nicholas Hilliard, and an older medieval tradition of manuscript illumination. Indeed *Elizabeth Freake and Daughter Mary* is a distant provincial echo of the courtly style that had developed in Northern Europe during the sixteenth century, a style that blended playful, colorful, linear, anti-classical Mannerism flowing northward from Italy with the indigenous and stylistically compatible Gothic tradition. The new stylistic amalgam reached a high point of development on the courtly level in England in the works of Hans Holbein. Filtering down through provincial strata, it finally arrived at this distillation in *Mrs. Freake and Daughter Mary* a century and a half later in Boston. Long after the European Baroque masters—Rubens and Rembrandt, Velasquez and Poussin—had lived and died, a flickering flame of the Middle Ages, fueled by Mannerism, still burned in the art as it did in the life of Colonial America.

The fragile early flowering of colorful decorative painting in Colonial America soon disappeared as more advanced styles became fashionable, although it was sufficiently durable to survive underground in American folk painting for two hundred years. Toward the end of the seventeenth century a group of portraits very different from those produced in Boston around 1670 appeared, including a *Self-Portrait* by Captain Thomas Smith, one of the masterpieces of early Baroque portraiture in America. The artist has learned something of chiaroscuro, and with a rather clumsy hand has brushed in shadows to give the head weight and substance. Gone are the delicate features of the earlier portraits. Not only does Smith employ modeling to define solid forms, but he also creates a three-dimensional ambience in which to set them. If we read this composition diagonally upwards, as we did with *Mrs. Freake and Daughter Mary*, our eye does not simply travel from area to area on the surface plane, but moves back step by step into pictorial space. A piece of paper inscribed with a poem is bent over the table edge in the lower left, serving as a space-defining device to lead the viewer into the composition. Smith's right hand is cupped over a skull, and the viewer's eye moves from it to the sitter's lace collar, his heavy head, the brass-studded upholstered chair, and a curtain. The background is no longer simply an abstract plane setting off the figure, but contains a window punched through the wall that allows the eye to proceed deeper into space to a scene of a harbor, fortress and battling ships.

The painting has gained a new dimension thematically as well as spatially. The man Thomas Smith is clearly more important than the costume and accouterments. The background scene presumably refers to an event in his career. The poem in the lower left ruminates on the fact that while we read the poem and study the likeness, Thomas Smith, creator of painting and poem who appears in the illusion of life before us, is in fact long dead, his well-fleshed head a skull like that on which his hand rests. The painting is a *Vanitas* portrait, a humbling reminder of our inevitable fate. Thomas Smith's *Self-Portrait*, with its solid forms and convincing space, marks the arrival of the Baroque style in America at the end of the century that had given it birth in Europe. Although Rubens and Van Dyck had worked in England during the 1620's and 30's, the general infusion of the Baroque into English art itself was long deferred by the Civil War and Puritan interregnum at mid-century. However with the return of Charles II and his court from continental exile in 1660, with the diffusion of Huguenot craftsmen and designers throughout the Protestant countries of Northern Europe after the Revocation of the Edict of Nantes ended religious toleration for Protestants in France in 1685, and finally with the Glorious Revolution of 1688 which brought William and Mary and their retinue from Holland to England, continental Baroque fashions and designs became naturalized in England, particularly on the court level. Transmission of the Baroque, diluted but recognizable, westward to the American colonies was facilitated when the restored English monarchy revoked the original commercial charters of the American colonies and issued new royal charters, setting up royal governors

Thomas Smith (active last quarter of 17th century). Self-Portrait, about 1690. (24½×23¾")
Owned by the Worcester Art Museum, Worcester, Massachusetts.

in provincial courts where the latest London fashions were introduced. In the colonies conditions were ripe for the acceptance of stylistic innovations as second and third generation Americans, bored with the Puritan rigidity of their forebears, wanted to begin to enjoy the fruits of the economic success they had gained.

In English painting a tradition of continental, especially German and Flemish, influence had been established by a succession of court painters from Holbein early in the sixteenth century through Rubens and Van Dyck early in the seventeenth century to Sir Peter Lely, an artist who appears to have been directly influential on Thomas Smith, at the end of the seventeenth century. However some continental stylistic influences came directly to the American colonies, by-passing England. For example, the Dutch had maintained their New Amsterdam colony until 1664, and a strong Dutch influence lingered long after the British

Anonymous. John Van Cortlandt, about 1731. (57×41″)
The Brooklyn Museum, Brooklyn, New York. Dick S. Ramsay Fund, 1941.

took it over and renamed it New York. Moreover one of the earliest trained Baroque artists to work in the American colonies was Justus Engelhardt Kühn (active 1708-1717), a German who emigrated to Annapolis, Maryland. Artists in the southern colonies, where the unit of settlement was the plantation rather than the town, were often itinerant. In about 1710 Kühn painted portraits of *Eleanor Darnall* and her brother, *Henry Darnall and His Colored Servant* (Maryland Historical Society, Baltimore, Maryland) at "The Woodyard," their family plantation in Prince George's County, Maryland. *Eleanor Darnall* stands on a checkered floor recalling seventeenth century children's portraits. Despite Baroque spatial pretensions, notably in the elaborate formal garden in the background, the girl and her dog are as flat as cardboard firescreens. Nevertheless such characteristic Baroque concerns as space, movement, contrast and rhythm, pervade the painting—the opening up of the background, the drapery and vine curving around the thick column, the bold turning of the balusters, the mask applied to the plinth, and the heavy massing of the floral arrangement. The large two-handled vase is an archetypal Baroque object, with the thick gadrooning pulsating as it marches around the body of the vessel, breaking up the surface into alternating and contrasting smooth and worked areas. Rhythmic echoes reverberate throughout the picture—two masks, a flower outside of the floral arrangement, the shape of the balusters, the movement of the gadrooning around the vase paralleling that of the drapery and vine around the column, and the repetitive balustrades and conical trees in the background.

During the years 1720-1740 an active school of portrait painters flourished in the Hudson River Valley of New York. As with the Boston limners a half century earlier, most of these itinerant artists remain anonymous. Although their portraits of members of patroon families use the vocabulary of Baroque painting, the bright color and emphasis on surface design recall the work of the earlier limners. This is evident in the charming anonymous portrait of *John Van Cortlandt*. At one time it was tempting for antiquarians to think of this scene as depicting a provincial American idyll, the fawn wandering out of the woods to be petted by a young American. However the entire composition is, in fact, based directly on a mezzotint after a painting by Sir Godfrey Kneller *(Lord Buckhurst and Lady Mary Sackville)*, a German who was the last and most influential of those continental artists who dominated English painting from the time of Holbein.

Engravings in general and mezzotints in particular were the dominant artistic influence on American painting in the eighteenth century, transmitting European designs to the colonies. This should not automatically condemn eighteenth century American art as imitative. According to eighteenth century artistic standards, still untouched by Romanticism's stress on individuality, adherence to tradition and the quotation from accepted sources was considered appropriate and desirable. The reliance upon European prints by American artists during the eighteenth century is of course a measure of their dependence, but also an index of the intensity of their aspirations. They wanted not only to produce pictures, but to produce the best possible pictures, to remain *au courant* with European art.

Despite the obvious advance represented by Captain Thomas Smith's Baroque *Self-Portrait* beyond the work of the earlier limners, subsequent stylistic advances in the first quarter of the eighteenth century were erratic. However, as the portrait of *John Van Cortlandt* already suggests, some of the best pictures were not the work of sophisticated artists but of provincials who used European sources as points of departure, and through a marriage of technical innocence and innate sensibility created fresh and striking images. The anonymous portrait of *Anne Pollard* is a case in point. As in the portrait of *John Van Cortlandt* the artist employs the outer forms of Baroque portraiture. Broad shadows are stroked in to model forms in space. The device of a painted oval or spandrel is used, its lower inside edge shadowed to interpose a painted wall between the viewer and the subject, making the illusion of pictorial space more convincing and relating it to the real space of the viewer. But despite the use of these space-enhancing devices, this delineation of a wizened centenarian, who had arrived in America as a child with the earliest Pilgrim settlers, is a surface arrangement of triangular and other shapes into a taut abstract pattern.

Justus Engelhardt Kühn (active 1708-1717). Eleanor Darnall, about 1710. (54×44½")
Collection of the Maryland Historical Society, Baltimore, Maryland.

Anonymous. Mrs. Anne Pollard, 1721. (28¾×24″)
Massachusetts Historical Society, Boston, Massachusetts.

One of the most important events in the history of American art was the arrival in the colonies early in 1729 of the first well-trained European artist, John Smibert (1688-1751). Smibert had been born in Edinburgh. After an early apprenticeship to a house painter, he went to London at the age of twenty-one to study art, supporting himself as a coach painter and by copying old master paintings. He subsequently spent more than three years in Italy (1717-1720), and from 1720-1728 was a competent if not outstanding London portraitist working in the manner of Sir Godfrey Kneller. Many of his commissions came from fellow Scots, and he apparently catered to a provincial clientele. When in 1728 Dean George Berkeley, later Bishop of Cloyne, embarked on a venture to found a new college in Bermuda, he persuaded Smibert to come along as professor of art and architecture. Smibert took with him his collections of prints, copies of old master paintings, and plaster casts of antique sculpture.

Berkeley's expedition landed at Newport, Rhode Island, and while it paused there to await further funds, Smibert painted a large group portrait of Berkeley and his party. The *Bermuda Group* was the first major painting produced in the American colonies, and one

the picture surface than in the character of the subject. He portrayed Isaac Royall as an icon, a person of a particular social position, a handsome, well-bred, self-confident, wealthy young man. There is little or no indication of character, of personality, of a human being with a sense of humor, a person ever racked by emotion or tormented by self-doubt.

During the mid-1740's Feke settled in Newport, Rhode Island, painting portraits there and on several occasions in Philadelphia. In 1748-1749 he reappeared in Boston, where he enjoyed an extraordinary spurt of artistic activity, producing a number of handsome three-quarter length portraits that rank among his most brilliant work. At mid-century Feke disappeared, quite inexplicably, and the field was left to a new generation of artists.

Painting in the southern and middle colonies was not altered by the appearance of a single major artist as was New England painting by the advent of Smibert. One of the earliest southern artists identifiable by name was Henrietta Johnston (active 1708-1728/29), a female pastelist in Charleston, South Carolina, the largest city in the South. Her small Baroque pastel portraits on paper have charm if not great artistic merit. Her successor as the leading Charleston artist during the colonial period was a Swiss, Jeremiah Theus (1719-1774), who painted sugary portraits, especially of women with pursed lips and pouter-pigeon poses, such as *Elizabeth Rothmaler* (Brooklyn Museum, Brooklyn, New York). The leading painter in Virginia was a London artist, Charles Bridges (active 1735-1740 in Virginia), who

Robert Feke (1705/10-after 1750). Isaac Royall and His Family, 1741. (56¼×77¾″)
Courtesy of the Harvard Law School, Cambridge, Massachusetts.

came to the colonies in his old age and received patronage from wealthy plantation families. In Maryland, Kühn was succeeded by a Swedish artist, Gustavus Hesselius (active 1711-1755) who departed from the usual restriction to portraiture to paint some interesting if not particularly attractive religious and mythological scenes. He also painted a few unusually sensitive portraits of Indians, *Tishcohan* and *Lapowinsa* (Historical Society of Pennsylvania, Philadelphia, Pennsylvania). His son, John Hesselius (1728-1778) became one of the most active portraitists in the Philadelphia-Annapolis area, but his style seems to have been influenced less by his father than by John Wollaston (active 1749-1767), a facile British artist who dominated the artistic scene in the middle and southern colonies at mid-century. Moderately skilled at painting drapery but woefully inept as a face painter, Wollaston nonetheless brought to the colonies firsthand experience of the contemporary Rococo style of Hudson and Highmore, sprightly and more colorful than Kneller's ponderous Baroque. Wollaston flattered his sitters through the decorative handling of drapery and landscape settings, but failed to convey a sense of the person portrayed. Indeed his art relied so heavily on stock pictorial devices that his sitters with their repetitive features all seem related.

A more pleasing, though less influential and productive, painter of Rococo portraits was William Williams (c. 1710-c. 1790) of Philadelphia who painted a delightful portrait of *Deborah Hall*, the daughter of Benjamin Franklin's printing partner. Although not much is known about Williams, the portrait speaks for his ability. In comparison with the Kühn portrait of *Eleanor Darnall* with its Baroque compactness of forms, tight curving movements, and repetitive rhythms, this Rococo portrait is much more linear, open and irregular. The sinuous descent of a tendril vine in front of a delicate plinth relief sculpture, and the free and asymmetrical pattern of the roses make a revealing stylistic contrast to the Baroque massing of flowers in Kühn's *Eleanor Darnall*.

Williams may have made a more significant contribution to American art through his early recognition and support of a young artist, Benjamin West (1738-1820). West was born and raised outside of Philadelphia, the son of a Quaker innkeeper. Williams, admiring West's youthful artistic precocity, loaned him books on art by Charles du Fresnoy and Jonathan Richardson which influenced West much more than did Williams' paintings. Unhappily the most obvious direct artistic influence on West's early style was exerted by John Wollaston. Fortunately West soon outstripped the superficial Wollaston. Even the early *Thomas Mifflin* (Historical Society of Pennsylvania, Philadelphia, Pennsylvania), painted in 1758 when West was only twenty, which reflects Wollaston's manner in the full jowls, almond eyes and dusky landscape setting, is far superior in its drawing, color, handling of space and light, and the balance of the composition to Wollaston's more static and pedestrian portraits.

West quickly achieved success as a portrait painter in Philadelphia, and his fame spread. But he was not satisfied with the prospect of a career as a portraitist in the American colonies. He had read glowing descriptions of the great art and artists of Europe in the books on art and art theory that Williams had given him. He learned that not all branches of painting were considered to be of equal importance, and that historical, religious and mythological pictures were the most highly regarded. Isolated in colonial America, his values shaped by his reading rather than by first-hand experience of great art, West burned with ambition to become a major artist. In response to his aspirations, a group of Philadelphia and New York businessmen sent West abroad to study in 1760, hoping to nourish the spark of artistic genius kindled in their country. West spent three years in Italy, and then settled in London where he soon achieved artistic eminence as history painter to George III and, eventually, President of the Royal Academy. Even though West never went back to America to yield a direct cultural return on the investment of his countrymen who had sent him abroad, he contributed enormously to the development of American painting. Throughout his long and distinguished career his London home and studio were at all times open to American artists, and as friend and teacher he exercised an important influence on several generations of American artists (see next chapter).

William Williams (about 1710-about 1790). Deborah Hall, 1766. (71¼×46½")
The Brooklyn Museum, Brooklyn, New York. Dick S. Ramsay Fund.

John Singleton Copley (1738-1815). Thaddeus Burr, 1758-1760. (50⅝×39⅞″)
City Art Museum, St. Louis, Missouri.

America's greatest colonial artist and a major artist by any standards, was John Singleton Copley (1738-1815). An exact contemporary of West, Copley was born in similarly modest circumstances, the son of a Boston tobacconist and his wife, recently arrived from Ireland. Copley grew up in Boston on Long Wharf, which jutted into the harbor. After his father's death on a trip to the West Indies, Copley's widowed mother, who continued to run the tobacco shop, married Peter Pelham, the engraver, in 1748. Through Pelham young Copley became familiar with the world of art and artists. He undoubtedly knew Pelham's friend, the aging Smibert, who lived nearby. He must have been aware of the recent work of Robert Feke, just then in a final blaze of productive glory in Boston. He may even have worked alongside of a promising young artist, John Greenwood (1727-1792), creator like Smibert and Feke of a large family group portrait, the *Greenwood-Lee Family* (Henry L. Shattuck, Brookline, Massachusetts), who may have been spending some time in Pelham's studio to learn the art of mezzotint engraving. Unfortunately for Copley, these stimulating halcyon days ended quickly. Pelham died in 1751, as did Smibert; Feke disappeared in 1750; and Greenwood for reasons as yet unknown departed in 1752 for Surinam, where he painted *Sea Captains Carousing at Surinam* (City Art Museum, St. Louis, Missouri), before proceeding to Holland and England and a career as an art dealer and auctioneer.

When Copley began his own career in 1753 at the age of fifteen, he faced little competition from such local artists as Smibert's son Nathaniel, who died in 1756 before his talent matured, or Joseph Badger (1708-1765), whose charming but unskilled paintings such as the portrait of his grandson, *James Badger* (Metropolitan Museum of Art New York, N.Y.) stand between the limners of the seventeenth century and the primitives of the nineteenth century in a continuing folk tradition. Copley's first major test arrived from England in the person of Joseph Blackburn (active 1753-1764 in America), an accomplished Rococo portraitist. Far from dismayed, Copley took advantage of the opportunity, learning all that he could from Blackburn, and like West with Wollaston, soon surpassed him. His portraits became increasingly deft and expressive, the Rococo style liberating his innate capabilities as a colorist. The bold and tasteful portrait of *Thaddeus Burr* with its spectacular brown-blue color harmony, painted when Copley was just over twenty, shows clearly why he rapidly achieved pre-eminence among American colonial artists. Although his success was guaranteed by technical competence alone, his real secret lay in his knowledge of his sitters and their requirements. Copley understood that what New Englanders valued in a portrait above all else was a good likeness. This was a pragmatic society, wedded to the facts of life, more concerned with the material realities of this world than the spiritual potentialities of the next. For this society portraiture was the one acceptable art form because it had a practical social application. A portrait could be sent to family far away as a token of the physical presence of a loved one, or it could descend to family distant in time, providing a kind of material immortality. In either case a good likeness was required, and Copley was able to produce just what his clients wanted. For example, early in his career he received a commission from Thomas Ainslie, Collector of the Port of Quebec, to paint portraits of Ainslie and his wife which, when completed, were sent to their respective parents in Scotland. Shortly thereafter the Ainslies' infant son went to Scotland to visit his grandparents. While having tea upon his arrival, the lad spotted his father's portrait on the dining room wall. He ran to it, and tried to grasp his father's hand. He called to the painted image, and when it did not respond, he stamped his foot and scolded it. The story, related by the delighted clients to Copley, testified to his accomplishment. Throughout the history of western art the feat of causing a viewer to believe that painted reality is actual reality has been the popular hallmark of artistic perfection. Conscious of his patrons' taste for realism, and able to satisfy it, Copley was flooded with commissions, especially from prosperous merchants like young Thaddeus Burr. As a result Copley himself grew wealthy. At the time of his marriage in 1769 to Susanna Clarke, daughter of a well-to-do Boston agent of the East India Company, Copley purchased a large estate on Beacon Hill adjoining the home of John Hancock, one of the richest men in New England.

Despite his success, Copley was not satisfied. It was all well and good to be the best artist in Boston, or even in America, but Copley, like Benjamin West, had read about great European artists. Never having seen their works, he yearned to know how his work stood in comparison. How did his art rate with that produced by the best contemporary artists in London? Consumed with curiosity and ambition, Copley sent the marvelous portrait of his half-brother, Henry Pelham, *The Boy with the Squirrel* (private collection) to London for exhibition at the Society of Artists in 1766. To his relief and pleasure, the painting was warmly received and won considerable praise. Benjamin West, delighted to discover the work of an American on exhibition in London, and Joshua Reynolds, the leading artist in Great Britain, sent helpful criticism and advice. They both encouraged Copley to come to Europe for at least a brief period of study. However Copley, pinned down by family responsibilities in Boston, felt unable to follow West's example and advice and go abroad.

In 1771 Copley received a letter from his former acquaintance and fellow artist, John Greenwood, now resident in London, commissioning a portrait of Greenwood's mother as she now appeared "with old age creeping upon her." Copley's portrait of Greenwood's mother, *Mrs. Humphrey Devereux*, is a masterpiece of his dramatic late American style. The subject is seated at a highly polished dropleaf table, a space-defining element between the viewer and the subject that is considerably more subtle and effective than the traditional painted oval spandrel. A flood of light illuminates the figure, casting part of the scene into deep shadow. Copley's art is marked by elements of style that characterize much provincial American art, although in his hands they are carried to unprecedented heights. For example, his light-dark contrasts are strong and crisp. American artists, far removed from collections of great master paintings and academies of art, received much of their awareness of art, their artistic training as it were, through the medium of black and white prints, especially mezzotints. In these, contrasts of light and dark are inevitably more pronounced than in the more subtly modulated original paintings. Carrying over the chiaroscuro of prints into their paintings, American artists often produced pictures marked by strong value contrasts. This seems to be one of the stylistic differences between American provincial painting and its European prototypes. Similarly Copley's notable sensitivity to color and his assertive use of line to demarcate color areas reveal a primary concern with the picture surface. Whether because of the lack of technical training to create the illusion of solid forms in real space or because of esthetic preference, it is a fact that much provincial art emphasizes surface design rather than three-dimensional illusion, and Copley's art, despite its impressive technical competence, is marked by this provincial mode of depiction. His work is clearly stamped by the general as well as artistic values of his society. Copley lovingly delineates textures; not since the Dutch masters of a century earlier had artists lavished as much care on the stuffs depicted. Like his Dutch predecessors, Copley was painting for a Protestant, mercantile, materialistic society, and his art was surely responsive to that society. Indeed Copley's great success as a portraitist lay not only in his ability to depict realistically the external appearances of people and their material surroundings, but also to capture the more profound realism of people as sentient human beings living out their lives in specific social contexts, whether as wealthy merchants, intellectual ministers, fruitful housewives, or characterful elders.

Despite Copley's great success, his American career was dramatically terminated by events beyond his control. Friend as well as painter of patriots like Paul Revere, Samuel Adams and John Hancock, and a man of genuinely democratic instincts, Copley nonetheless had risen into lofty social and economic circles. His family by marriage and most of his newer friends were distinctly loyalist. As the tension grew between England and her American colonies, Copley found it increasingly difficult to maintain a firm straddle on the political fence. Bad times politically meant bad times for the artist, as potential clients were diverted to other concerns. In 1774, after the Boston Tea Party, portrait commissions having fallen off sharply, Copley finally sailed from the American colonies to fulfill his long-cherished dream of a trip to Europe and a chance to study the works of old and modern

John Singleton Copley (1738-1815). Mrs. Humphrey Devereux, 1771. (40⅛×32″)
National Art Gallery, Wellington, New Zealand.

Ralph Earl (1751-1801). Roger Sherman, about 1777. (64¾×49½")
Yale University Art Gallery, New Haven, Connecticut. Gift of Roger Sherman White, January 1918.

masters. While he was in Italy, war broke out at home at Lexington and Concord. Copley was reunited with his family in London, and there soon gained considerable success as a history painter (see next chapter). He never returned to his native land.

Although Copley left America, the paintings he left behind exercised a marked influence on subsequent painting in New England. The one picture known to have been produced by the Connecticut artist, Ralph Earl (1751-1801), before he left for England in 1778, a portrait of *Roger Sherman*, is Earl's masterpiece, one of the most impressive of all American paintings, and clearly reflective of the benign influence of Copley. Tastefully subdued in color, the painting depicts Sherman sitting in a painted Windsor chair, a compositional device occasionally used by Copley in his late American paintings. However Copley never invoked such an open composition, the sitter facing the viewer, and only rarely would he portray a full figure seated; his seated figures are usually shown at three-quarters length. In *Roger Sherman* the composition is supported firmly by the sitter's legs thrust in one direction balancing two chair legs that splay out in the other. The arms of the Windsor curving back in space echo the movement of Sherman's arms and shoulders. The relationship between foreground and background planes is established linearly as was common with Feke; here the lines where walls meet floor are picked up by the lines of the bottom of Sherman's waistcoat. The triangles formed by thumb and forefinger on each hand and the similarly shaped wedge of white cravat peeking through the waistcoat, along with the edges of the jacket and the rows of buttons and buttonholes, march one's eye irresistibly to Sherman's stern but kindly face, the focal point of the portrait. The sober and restrained style reinforces awareness of the character of the sitter, a self-made man who worked his way up as shoemaker, surveyor, and lawyer to become Judge of the Connecticut Superior Court. He was a delegate to the Continental Congress, attended the Constitutional Convention, and served in the United States Congress as both a Representative and as a Senator. He was one of only two men (the other was Robert Morris of Pennsylvania) to sign the Declaration of Independence, the Articles of Confederation, and the Federal Constitution, the three major documents of American independence. The slightly primitive quality of the angular portrait enhances rather than detracts from the impression of strength, spare toughness and moral rectitude. *Roger Sherman* is an unforgettable symbol of the spirit of independence and the will to achieve and preserve it that marked the establishment of the United States of America as a self-reliant federal republic, and the end of the colonial period.

John Trumbull (1756-1843). The Declaration of Independence (detail), 1786-1797.
Yale University Art Gallery, New Haven, Connecticut.

The Federal Period:
Americans at Home and Abroad

EIGHTEENTH century Americans who thought about art were of two minds about it. On the one hand feelings of national pride disposed them to believe that America would one day become a center for the arts. Early in the century Bishop Berkeley had formulated a theory, repeated later by Benjamin Franklin, that the arts move westward. This theory noted that art had first been centered in the Eastern Mediterranean basin, then flowered in Greece, moved to Rome and, after the hiatus of the "dark ages," continued on from Renaissance Italy to France. Now, in the eighteenth century, England was arriving at pre-eminence, and it was logical to assume that the next step to the West would make the new world the next center for the arts.

In opposition to this chauvinistic confidence that the arts would someday flourish in America was a deeply-rooted pragmatic American attitude that relegated the impractical arts to the periphery of American life. After the American Revolution the tendency to dismiss the arts as irrelevant was reinforced by a positive conviction that art, which in its sensual appeal stimulated the emotions rather than the intellect, was corrupting, and therefore to be avoided.

American artists were whipsawed between these two points of view. Again and again the situation recurred in which a promising young American artist, wishing to travel to Europe to study art, would be sent abroad by public-minded citizens intending their subsidy of the artist as an investment in America's cultural future. The artist would spend years in Europe studying, expanding the range and vocabulary of his art. On his return to America he would find that despite his early encouragement, there was in fact no patronage for the ambitious art that he now wished to produce—history pictures, mythology, landscapes. Portraiture was the only art form for which there was a continuing demand in pragmatic America, and through the first third of the nineteenth century, the artist who hoped to make a living by painting anything other than portraits was tilting at windmills.

Despite the discouraging obstacles that artists faced in the new world, scores and eventually hundreds of young Americans still wanted to become artists and found the financial support necessary to get to Europe to study. Many remained there as expatriates, from Copley and West to James McNeill Whistler, John Singer Sargent and Mary Cassatt. But more returned to America, their work enriched by what they had learned in Europe.

For over half a century the dominant influence on American artists abroad was that of Benjamin West. When West arrived in London in 1763 after three years of study in Italy, he decided to make his career there rather than return to America, and sent to Philadelphia

Matthew Pratt (1734-1805). The American School, 1765. (36×50¼″)
The Metropolitan Museum of Art, New York. Gift of Samuel P. Avery, 1897.

for his fiancée, Elizabeth Shewall. Among the friends who escorted her to London for the wedding was a young Philadelphia artist, Matthew Pratt, who remained to become one of West's first American pupils. West's studio rapidly became an important training center for American artists, a fact celebrated in Pratt's memorable *The American School*, a view of the studio in 1765. Most of the figures, other than West standing at the left, are unidentified, although one, probably the artist at the easel, is Pratt himself and another may be the New York artist, Abraham Delanoy, also one of West's early pupils. They were soon followed by Charles Willson Peale, Gilbert Stuart, John Trumbull and a host of others.

While West's effectiveness as a teacher resulted from his magnetic and kindly personality, his importance flowed from his perceptive view of art and its meaning in his time. If to twentieth century eyes his paintings seem static, dull, and occasionally pompous, it is obvious from the fact that so many young artists found his art and his thinking provocative and stimulating that he requires careful study, particularly within the context of the artistic values of his own day.

As a youth in America, his imagination stimulated by the books on art he had read, West was stirred by a desire to become not just an artist but a master of the highest branch of art, a painter of historical subjects. In Italy he was caught up in the powerful surge of interest in classical antiquity that pervaded the intellectual climate of the day. Influential writings of the rationalist philosophers of the Enlightenment were suggesting that man, in

opposition to the traditional Christian belief in taint by original sin, was essentially pure, and had simply been debased over the centuries by corrupt institutions of church and state. If eighteenth century man could divest himself of these corrupt institutions, he could then construct a better society. As living proof of the inherent purity of man, writers like Rousseau pointed to natural man, man in a savage or uncivilized state, such as the American Indian. With some prodigious misreading of available evidence, philosophers of the Enlightenment found in the American Indian an example of a society of naturally good men practicing all of the civic and family virtues. They also postulated that history provided similar evidence of the creative potential of unspoiled man; in classical Greece and Rome, before corrupt institutions had arisen, man had created ideal societies where the highest standards of justice, virtue, courage, beauty, morality and every imaginable social good obtained. Civilization had declined ever since, but classical antiquity demonstrated what man could achieve when free of corruption, providing a model for eighteenth century man as he worked to rebuild his own society. It was therefore obviously important to discover as much as possible about antiquity. As a result the eighteenth century turned to the classical past not out of a dry and dusty antiquarian curiosity, but out of an intense desire, born of potent social and political ideas that before the end of the century would bring revolution in America and France, to reach back across the centuries and touch hands with the past. At Pompeii and Herculaneum the earth was scraped away to reveal the remains of the Roman world beneath; the Greek temples at Paestum claimed new attention; the *Ruins of the Palace of the Emperor Diocletian at Spalato* were carefully measured and published in 1764 by Robert Adam; James Stuart and Nicholas Revett published precise and beautiful measured drawings of *The Antiquities of Athens* in 1762; and even earlier Robert Wood published the *Ruins of Palmyra* (1753) and *Balbec* (1757). In Rome itself a prime mover behind the whole classical vogue was the German Johann Joachim Winckelmann. Through such writings as *Gedanken über die Nachahmung der griechischen Werke in der Malerei und Bildhauerkunst* (1755), translated into English by Fuseli in 1765, and *Geschichte der Kunst des Altertums* (1764), and through his artistic protégé, Anton Raphael Mengs, he exercised enormous influence.

And there in Italy from 1760 to 1763, right in the midst of this exciting rediscovery of the past, was Benjamin West, an alert and receptive young provincial from Philadelphia. A few years later West began to weave these new ideas and discoveries into the fabric of his art. *Agrippina Landing at Brundisium with the Ashes of Germanicus* (1768) asserts the importance of classical antiquity as a model for the eighteenth century. Germanicus was a Roman hero, treacherously assassinated by a political rival. On one level the picture is a tribute to a hero who has sacrificed his life for his country—*dulce et decorum est pro patria mori*. But more importantly it dramatizes the admirable performance of Agrippina carrying her husband's ashes in a cinerary urn and followed by grieving children. Her courage, stoicism and dignity in the face of tragic circumstances, normative behavior in classical times, is presented here to inspire emulation.

The presentation of a Roman subject and a moralizing message is not unusual in eighteenth century painting; what is significantly new and different is that West attempts to depict the Roman subject in accurate Roman terms, making the painting as realistic as he could. The central cortege, obviously based on relief sculpture in its flat disposition of figures and its monochromy, following the injunctions of Winckelmann to the letter, was in fact specifically based on a published detail of the procession of senators and their wives from the *Ara Pacis*. The arcaded façade in the background was taken directly from Robert Adam's recent *Ruins of the Palace of the Emperor Diocletian at Spalato* (1764). The triangularly composed grieving group on the left is obviously reminiscent of classical pedimental sculpture.

West also used a dramatic theatrical composition to communicate his didactic message to maximum effect. The main action in the center of the stage is strongly lit, with supporting groups in the wings to frame and define the action. A secular sermon in paint to

Benjamin West (1738-1820). Agrippina Landing at Brundisium with the Ashes of Germanicus, 1768. (64½×106½″)
Yale University Art Gallery, New Haven, Connecticut. Gift of Louis M. Rabinowitz.

an eighteenth century audience, *Agrippina* prefigures French Neo-classicism, notably the paintings of Jacques-Louis David, in the political implications of its call for a change in the values and standards of contemporary society, in its concern for historical accuracy and realism, and in the new classicism of its sculptural, coloristically muted style.

Like *Agrippina*, *The Death of General Wolfe*, exhibited by West in 1771, treats the theme of the death of a hero. However in this case the death scene is actually represented, and the subject is taken from the recent past rather than from classical antiquity. General Wolfe died on September 13, 1759, on the Plains of Abraham, outside of Quebec, in the war against the French. The innovations in thematic seriousness and pictorial realism initiated in *Agrippina* are here carried forward to achieve what has been termed a "revolution in history painting," as West depicted the figures in contemporary dress (against the advice of Joshua Reynolds and George III). Although contemporary subject matter was not unusual, modern dress was. History paintings as a matter of course treated contemporary themes allegorically, with the figures draped in togas, amidst soaring angelic choirs or the shades of heroic predecessors. Classical dress and details helped to demonstrate that the hero and his deeds transcended ordinary life and were worthy of the ancients. In *The Death of Wolfe* West inverted the emphasis, stressing the contemporaneity of it all. This man who heroically gives his life for his country, is an eighteenth century Englishman; the heroism, courage and dignity he demonstrates, these classical virtues, are in fact eighteenth century realities.

West is preaching again, using a variety of devices to help deliver his sermon. The composition remains theatrical, with highlighted drama in the center stage supported by flanking groups. A knowledgeable eighteenth century connoisseur would have found this painting suffused with subtle pictorial references. The placement of the figure of Wolfe with a draped flag behind him recalls countless compositions of the descent of Christ from the cross. Wolfe's comrades mournfully support his body in a compositional echo of a traditional "Lamentation" over the body of Christ. On the right a young officer wrings his hands in the pose of a youthful St. John the Evangelist at the Crucifixion, while on the left a wounded officer recoils into a pocket of figures like a swooning Virgin Mary. *The Death of Wolfe* thus invokes a rich substratum of Christian iconography, subtly using compositional Crucifixion, Deposition and Lamentation echoes to imply parallels between the death of Wolfe and the martyrdom of Christ.

In the left foreground a seated Indian contemplates the scene. A natural man, a noble savage, he seems most fully aware of the meaning of Wolfe's sacrifice. West, pulling out all of the stops to intensify the contemporary viewer's response to the painting, was very much aware of European fascination with Indians. Earlier, in Italy, a young artist fresh from the land of the noble savages, West had been taken by a group of Roman *cognoscenti*, including Cardinal Albani, to view the *Apollo Belvedere*. As his eyes fell on the famous antique sculpture, West gasped, with apparent but unlikely spontaneity, "My God, how like a

Benjamin West (1738-1820). The Death of General Wolfe, 1770. (59½×84″)
The National Gallery of Canada, Ottawa, Ontario. Canadian War Memorials Collection.

Mohawk warrior." Perfect! The youth from the forests of the new world seemed to grasp instinctively the parallel between the godlike classical figure and natural man, the noble savage unspoiled by civilization. West capitalized on European interest in the American Indian in a number of paintings, notably in his next major modern history painting, a depiction of William Penn's *Peace Treaty with the Indians* (Independence Hall, Philadelphia, Pennsylvania), exhibited at the Royal Academy in 1772. Turning to advantage his own Pennsylvania Quaker background as well as his first-hand knowledge of Indians, he presented Penn's "Holy Experiment" in Pennsylvania as evidence in fulfilment both of Rationalist philosophy and biblical prophecy that men of good will could create a new society, that the lion and the lamb, here in the persons of white man and red man, could lie down and dwell together in peace and harmony, and had done so on the banks of the Delaware.

West's innovations and accomplishments as a history painter greatly impressed his fellow colonial, John Singleton Copley. When Copley arrived in England in 1774, aspiring like West before him to go beyond portraiture and become a history painter, he perceived that West had significantly advanced the course of history painting with his realism. Copley first won recognition as an artist in England with his exhibition of *Watson and the Shark* in 1778 at the Royal Academy. Instead of the death of a hero, *Watson and the Shark* represents the bizarre maiming of a youth. Brooke Watson, a prosperous shipper and later Lord Mayor of London, as a boy had served as a midshipman aboard an English ship. On one occasion, while the vessel was anchored in Havana harbor, Watson went swimming and was attacked by a shark. On its first strike the shark had stripped all of the flesh from Watson's leg below the knee. It then returned and snapped off his foot at the ankle. As the shark closed once more to devour its helpless victim, Watson's shipmates came to the rescue. This is the climactic moment that Copley depicts. Like West in *The Death of Wolfe*, Copley portrays a scene that is recent in time but distant in setting, cushioning the impact of the straightforward presentation of a contemporary event in contemporary costume on English viewers unaccustomed to such immediacy. But Copley goes beyond West in heightening the realism by not only using modern dress but also presenting an actual view of Havana harbor, based on engravings, so that such landmarks as Morro Castle, the cathedral, and the convent towers are readily identifiable.

Watson and the Shark is more directly *reportage* than *The Death of Wolfe*, without complex classical, religious or philosophical overtones, although the figure of Watson is based on the *Borghese Warrior*, evocative of gladiatorial combat between warrior and beast. The painting may not be profound, but it is effective. The composition is held together by a zigzag movement through the shark and boy, boat and background, both on the picture surface and plunging deep into pictorial space. Dramatic lighting emphasizes the boy, the shark, and the man with the boathook. It calls specific attention to the tip of the hook, reinforced by a triangular wedge of light on the stem of the boat, and to the nose of the shark. There is a sense of pending but uncertain impact. Will the men in the boat grasp the boy before the shark gets him? Will the boathook stop the shark? All is held in suspense. The scene is tautly bound within a pyramidal arrangement, and despite its transitory nature, is locked in place forever.

This monumental painting has sometimes been considered an important example of proto-Romanticism, anticipating such later works as Géricault's *Raft of the Medusa. Watson* does indeed reflect that eighteenth century fascination with the exotic and the horrible that forms part of the root structure of Romanticism, but the picture is quite orthodox in its composition. Nineteenth century artists may well have been aware of the painting, but Copley exercised more influence on David and French Neo-classicism through his realistic, portrait-filled history pictures. Instead it was Benjamin West, always sensitive to artistic novelty, who painted romantic pictures as early as the 1770's with *Saul and the Witch of Endor* (Wadsworth Atheneum, Hartford, Connecticut) and the *Cave of Despair* (Mr. and Mrs. Paul Mellon), and whose *Death on a Pale Horse* (Philadelphia Museum of Art, Philadelphia, Pennsylvania), exhibited in Paris in 1803, directly influenced French romantic painters.

In *The Death of the Earl of Chatham* (1779-1781, Tate Gallery, London), Copley carried realism a step further by depicting an important event that was local as well as contemporary. Fifty-five portraits of individuals present at the event, accurately set in the House of Lords, are woven into a complex composition. Although the picture may seem static now, filled with so many portraits, it was produced in a pre-camera era when people were eager to see pictures of important events. Today's viewer is no longer familiar with the people portrayed or the complexities of their relationships, but to Copley's contemporaries the painting represented a rich interplay of political positions, party antipathies, personal scandals, and family backgrounds.

Copley's next history painting, *The Death of Major Peirson* (1782-1784) marked the zenith of his career. On the night of January 5/6, a French detachment of nine hundred troops had invaded the Channel isle of Jersey. Aided by surprise, the French quickly gained control of the capital city of St. Helier. However before they could secure the island, a twenty-four year old British officer, Major Francis Peirson, rallied the local militia and the remaining British forces and launched a counterattack that swept back into St. Helier. In a bloody pitched battle the English regained the city and the island. At the moment of victory, Major Peirson was slain.

The Death of Major Peirson achieved considerable popular success when it was exhibited in 1784. The spirited character of the scene is enhanced by the vigor of the composition, the brilliance and boldness of the color, and the surface flicker of light and dark contrasts. Years later the Duke of Wellington observed that this exciting picture, smoke-obscured and filled with the sounds, smell and stir of combat, with troops marching, banners flying, and civilians fleeing, was the only painting that he had ever found convincingly evocative of the real feel of battle. The subject of the painting also contributed greatly to its popular success. England had endured a long period of war marked by few victories. News from America was not good, and even success in the colonies involved Englishmen killing Englishmen. But a victory over a traditional continental foe, the French, was a different matter, and on Jersey the triumph was made all the more gratifying in that it had been snatched from the jaws of defeat. The poignant death of a youthful hero cut down at his moment of glory, the retribution exacted by a faithful Negro servant, and the selfless devotion of the mortally wounded drummer who ignores his own wounds to turn toward his lost leader, all added to the picture's appeal. Modern viewers may find this arrangement of figures in costume theatrical; indeed a creative act of imagination is required to comprehend the impact this picture had in its own day. Within the context of a time when visual images were still uncommon, one must imagine this as a contemporary street scene with soldiers and civilians in modern dress, with death and destruction all around, and terrified civilians fleeing. Copley stressed the immediacy of the terror by using members of his own family for the group on the right, including his wife with upraised arms and a son, John Singleton Copley, Jr., the little boy with the hat, later Lord Chancellor of England.

The Death of Major Peirson, like *Watson and the Shark*, has a realistic setting; the town square of St. Helier is accurately depicted, including the statue of George II in front of city hall and Town Hill on the left. The painting also follows *Watson* in the incorporation of a Negro as a dramatic central figure. As in *The Death of Chatham*, the composition centers around a death group and includes portraits of people who participated in the event.

In his large history paintings Copley completed the "revolution" begun by West, recording contemporary events with increasing realism of dress, setting, action and the portrayal of individuals present. The innovative impulse of West and Copley toward realism, not to be found in the work of their English contemporaries, may have reflected pragmatic and materialistic values of the provincial society from which they had sprung (the realism of Copley's American portraits as responsive to the values of his society has already been noted). If so, their achievement as history painters in England may stand as perhaps the earliest instance of an identifiable American contribution to the development of European art, and indeed one of the earliest American contributions to European culture.

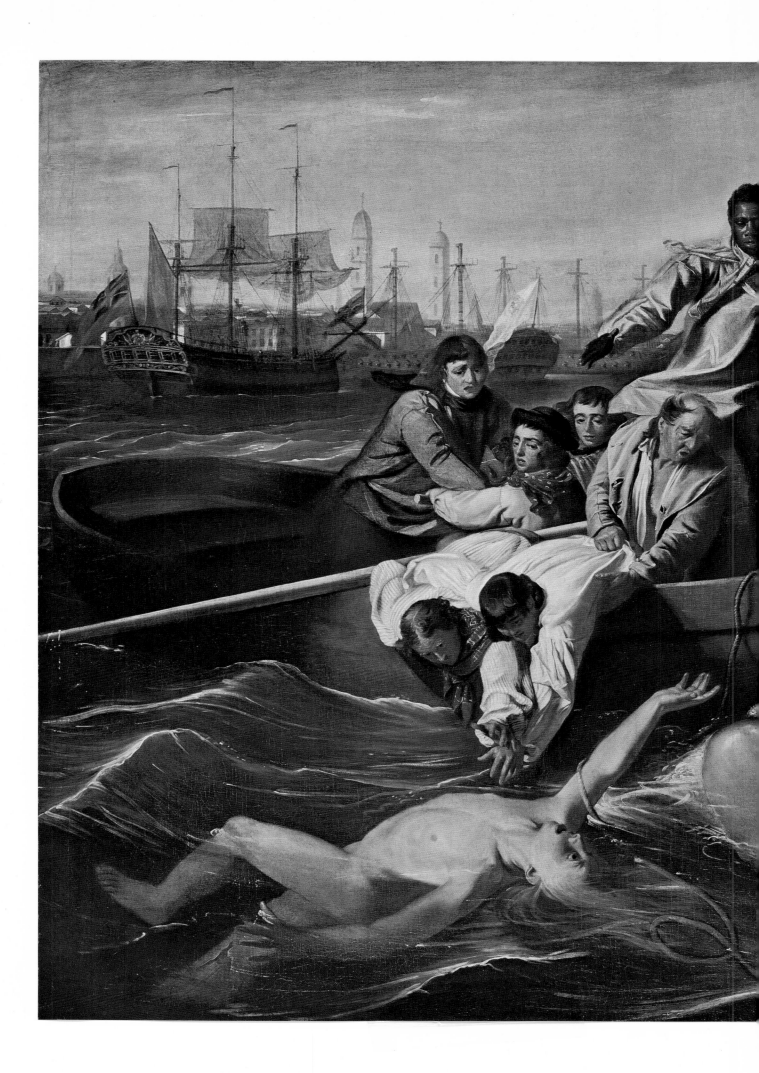

John Singleton Copley (1738-1815).
Watson and the Shark, 1778. (72×90⅛″)
Courtesy, Museum of Fine Arts, Boston, Massachusetts.
Gift of Mrs. George von Lengerke Meyer.

John Singleton Copley (1738-1815). The Death of Major Peirson, 1782-1784. (97×144″)

By Courtesy of the Trustees, The Tate Gallery, London.

Copley's one artistic descendant, although not his pupil, was John Trumbull (1756-1843). Trumbull was born in Lebanon, Connecticut, to a prominent, well-to-do family (his father became Governor of Connecticut during the Revolution). His youthful desire to study with Copley in Boston and become a painter was frustrated by his family. While at Harvard College he did meet Copley and was strongly influenced by his work. He graduated from Harvard in 1773. When the American Revolution began, Trumbull joined the Continental Army, using his artistic talent to draw maps and sketches of British positions. He served briefly as aide-de-camp to General George Washington, a fact of which he boasted until his dying day. After a petty dispute over the date of his commission, he quit the army. Renting John Smibert's old studio in Boston, he copied some of Smibert's copies of old master paintings and also painted portraits and history pictures that reflect the influence of Copley. In 1780 he went to London to study with Benjamin West. However upon the arrest and execution in America of the British spy, Major John André, Trumbull, an ex-officer in the Revolutionary Army, was jailed in reprisal. He was released in 1781 (Copley and West posted his bail), and deported to America. When hostilities ended, he returned to London to resume his study, arriving just as Copley's *Death of Major Peirson* was exhibited to popular acclaim. He realized that West and Copley had moved the most important branch of art, history painting, into new ground with their increased realism. He also realized that there was an important category of contemporary history, the American Revolution, inappropriate for use by West and Copley as Americans living permanently in England. With the

46

encouragement of West and Copley, Trumbull undertook a series of Revolutionary War scenes. The first of these, *The Death of General Warren at Bunker's Hill* (Yale University Art Gallery, New Haven, Connecticut), with its central death group, waving banners, diagonal shafts of fire and smoke, a prominently placed Negro servant, and a fleeing group on the right, is clearly derived from Copley's *Death of Major Peirson*. The second, *The Death of General Montgomery at Quebec* (Yale University Art Gallery, New Haven, Connecticut) is patterned on West's *Death of General Wolfe*, which earlier represented a general's death at Quebec, and includes an Indian, a grieving figure holding his wrist and other similarities. In 1785 Trumbull was invited by Thomas Jefferson, the first American minister to France, to visit Paris, where Trumbull was obviously influenced by French Neo-classicism. The third picture in the series, *The Declaration of Independence*, which he began in Paris, assisted by factual advice from Jefferson who was a participant, is much more neo-classical in its balance and order than the earlier, intensely movemented battle scenes. This results in part, of course, from the subject itself which, like Copley's *Death of Chatham*, involves an interior setting with lots of figures, necessarily leading to static rows of heads. However the scene represents one of the crowning moments of the Enlightenment, as new world men declared themselves independent from an old and unresponsive regime, affirming their resolve to construct a new society based on reason rather than on tradition and empty forms. The balance, repose and stability of the painting echoes the rationality of the enterprise.

In all Trumbull completed a total of eight Revolutionary war scenes, traveling extensively throughout America to sketch the sites and to take life portraits of participants. Since West and Copley never returned to America, it was Trumbull who applied their innovations to American subjects, and re-introduced the accomplishments of these American artists into the mainstream of American art.

When Trumbull had first arrived in London in 1780 he was welcomed and introduced to the mysteries of West's studio by a young American painter, Gilbert Stuart (1755-1828), West's apprentice and principal assistant. Stuart was born in Narragansett, Rhode Island. His father had come from Scotland to establish a snuff mill for Dr. Thomas Moffatt, John Smibert's nephew and a member of Berkeley's expedition, depicted next to Smibert in *The Bermuda Group*. When the snuff venture failed, the Stuart family moved to Newport, where young Stuart became exposed to art in the small private collections of Moffatt and William Hunter. In 1769 a Scottish portrait painter, Cosmo Alexander (c. 1724-1772), arrived in Newport. After a brief stay he returned to Scotland, taking Stuart with him. Upon Alexander's sudden and untimely death, Stuart was cast loose in Edinburgh. He managed to work his way back to America, but the experience at sea was brutal; in subsequent years the normally loquacious Stuart never touched upon the subject.

Upon the outbreak of the American Revolution, Stuart's loyalist family left Newport for Nova Scotia. Stuart himself went to London in 1775 to pursue his artistic career. Intending like Ralph Earl to paint, not to study, he almost starved to death before he swallowed his pride after a year and applied to Benjamin West for help. West took him in as a pupil and assistant. In 1777 Stuart began to exhibit at the Royal Academy, and during the next few years, while he continued to work with West, he exhibited regularly. Stuart attracted little attention at the Academy until 1782, when he exhibited four paintings that were well received, especially a splendid full-length portrait of a Scottish client, Mr. Grant of Congalton, a painting more popularly known as *The Skater*.

Stuart differed from West, Copley and Trumbull in that he had no wish to paint history pictures. Portraits were his forte. He loved to paint faces, to "pin the sitter's head to the canvas," to capture the aspect and personality of the subject. The remaining parts of painting bored him as hack work to be discharged as expeditiously as possible. As a result he painted very few full-length portraits, which led to allegations that he could not paint below the shirt buttons. However *The Skater* provides convincing proof that Stuart could paint superb full-length portraits when he chose. *The Skater* is painted in a cool harmony of gray,

green-gray, black and white with touches of red in the background. The head, a strong area of flesh color framed by a jaunty black hat and silhouetted against the light gray winter sky, serves as the focal point for the entire composition. The arrangement invokes a precarious formal balance between stability and movement that subtly suggests the essence of skating. The skater glides away from the stable verticals of the tree and leaning figures on the right. A small figure in a red jacket, sitting on the bank of the frozen river to tie his skates, makes the transition between tree and skater, between land and river, between stability and motion. On the left the clockwise movement of circling skaters imparts a pull to the left, away from the shore, on the main figure. The composition is at rest at the top and on the right, in motion to the left and at the bottom. The primary movement from right to left is bracketed by a counterpoint of movements curving into space; the bend of the road away from the scene in the background, and the curl cut in the ice as the skater turns toward the viewer. With arms folded as he glides, the skater evokes an allegorical image of Winter as one of the Four Seasons, arms buried in a muffler, hugging his body against the cold. After *The Skater* was exhibited, it disappeared from view until 1878 when it was again shown at the Academy. In the interim the name of Stuart had become dissociated from the picture. In a flurry of attributions it was first suggested that the painting was by Gainsborough, then Romney, then Raeburn, until Stuart was finally identified as the artist through connection with the original exhibition record.

In 1783 Stuart moved out of West's studio to pursue his own career. He soon achieved a rank among the leading portraitists of the day just behind Reynolds, Gainsborough and Romney. Commissions flowed in, and Stuart, who had known intense poverty and deprivation, plunged himself into an orgy of self-indulgence. He was a dandy in dress, and delighted in lavish entertainments where, over quantities of food and drink, he amused his friends as a brilliant raconteur. Although he earned a substantial income, his expenses rose even more rapidly, especially after his marriage in 1786, and his extravagance induced constant and severe financial strain. As with most portrait painters, Stuart's procedure on receipt of a commission was to collect half of his fee in advance. His need for money tempted him to begin more pictures than he could hope to finish, a procedure to which he was further inclined by the fact that it was the initial phase of portrait painting, the taking of the likeness, that interested him most. It became increasingly difficult for him to finish a portrait.

Stuart suddenly resolved his problems in 1787 by leaving London, going to Dublin where he worked for five years. In Ireland he followed the same pattern of extravagant living. Despite the flood of commissions that came his way as the best portrait painter in Ireland, Stuart's financial situation deteriorated to the point where he saw the inside of a debtor's prison. However the canny Stuart was not without hope or resources. As an American with a detached view of America, he saw clearly that George Washington, as commanding general of the victorious Continental Army and as first President of the United States, had achieved legendary stature in his own lifetime. Stuart reasoned that there would be an endless demand for likenesses of Washington, and if he could only get access to the President and persuade him to sit, he could secure a steady income by selling copies of his portrait and by publishing an engraving of it. As for the moral question of abandoning a large number of unfinished paintings in Ireland, paintings begun in order to collect the initial half fee, Stuart rationalized that he would in fact be performing a good deed since completing the portraits would provide welcome employment for local Irish artists who had suffered from his competition.

Stuart returned to America early in 1793, establishing a studio in New York. At the time of his return, the arts in America were at a low ebb. Several of the best American artists, including West and Copley, had left before the war and never returned. Those who did return found that patronage was severely limited by a depressed economy. Times were difficult, and even such good artists as Matthew Pratt in Philadelphia were reduced to painting signs. However among the social elite in America, especially those associated with Washington's new regime who formed a Federalist aristocracy, there continued to be a

Gilbert Stuart (1755-1828). The Skater, 1782. (96⅝×58⅛″)
National Gallery of Art, Washington, D.C. Andrew Mellon Collection.

demand for portraits. Moreover Stuart was a far more accomplished painter than any of his American rivals. His early New York portraits, such as *Mrs. Richard Yates* (National Gallery of Art, Washington, D.C.), were the equal of high style London portraits, and established Stuart's artistic primacy. In 1795 Stuart followed the federal government from New York to Philadelphia. Armed with a letter of introduction from John Jay, a satisfied client, Stuart gained access to President Washington and painted his first portrait of him. This was the so-called "Vaughan" portrait which shows Washington facing right. Although the "Vaughan" Washington is thought to have been destroyed, the version at the National Gallery of Art, Washington, D.C., may be the original version, and many other replicas survive. Stuart, while painting a portrait, would utilize his conversational brilliance to engage the interest of his sitters, and animate their expressions. However he was unable to arouse any response from Washington who, apparently in pain from ill-fitting false teeth, sat in stony silence while Stuart enthusiastically but futilely turned the one-sided conversation to horses, war, farming and other subjects of possible interest.

Dissatisfied with the "Vaughan" portrait, Stuart was happy to receive a commission the following year from Lord Lansdowne in England for a full-length portrait of Washington. Shortly afterward, commissioned by Martha Washington to paint a portrait of her husband, Stuart produced a bust-length variant of the "Lansdowne" picture. Known as the "Athenaeum" *Washington*, this is the finest of the three Washington portraits Stuart painted, and is the likeness by which Washington is best known to posterity. Having finally gotten a good likeness, Stuart was reluctant to complete the portrait and deliver it to Martha Washington. Instead he used it as the source for an endless stream of copies, jokingly referred to by Stuart as his "hundred dollar bills," that he cranked out to meet the demand for Washington portraits. By the time of Stuart's death, when his widow sold the painting to a committee which presented it to the Boston Athenaeum, it still had not been completed. Stuart had "pinned the likeness to the canvas," and that was what he cared about.

One reason why Stuart was so reluctant to surrender the profitable "Athenaeum" portrait was his disappointment in regard to an engraved likeness of Washington. He had planned to publish an engraving after one of his Washington portraits anticipating that it would yield a considerable income. Without Stuart's knowledge, Lord Lansdowne gave permission to a London engraver, James Heath, to engrave the "Lansdowne" *Washington*. Heath's engraving could not have been more timely; it was published at the beginning of 1800, immediately following Washington's death in the final month of the old century. It capitalized on a surge of interest both in America and Europe in portraits of the lamented leader, and Stuart, with no copyright laws to protect him, gained not a penny.

Despite this disappointment, Stuart enjoyed considerable patronage and prospered. The fashionable flocked to his studio in Germantown, outside of Philadelphia. In 1803 he moved to Washington, again following the seat of government, and painted there such important political figures as James Madison, John Adams and Thomas Jefferson. Chronicler of the faces of the founding fathers, Stuart is perhaps the best known of all American painters.

Stuart returned to his native New England in 1805 at the age of fifty, settling in Boston to spend the rest of his life. Stuart liked Boston and Boston liked him. Still addicted to good food, good drink and good conversation, although less extravagantly than in earlier days, the convivial Stuart became the grand old man of American painting. He welcomed a steady stream of young artists who came to Boston to seek his advice and his instruction, and his influence dominated American portraiture deep into the nineteenth century.

If Stuart painted the best and most familiar portraits of George Washington, he lagged far behind Charles Willson Peale (1741-1827), in the number of Washington life portraits. Washington sat for Peale no less than seven times. During his early years in Annapolis, Maryland, Peale was a saddler, a watch and clock maker, and a silversmith. In 1763, convinced upon seeing the uninspired work of an itinerant portrait painter that he could do better, Peale exchanged a saddle for some painting lessons from John Hesselius. Later he

Gilbert Stuart (1755-1828). The Athenaeum Portrait of George Washington, 1796. (39⅝×34½″)
Courtesy, Museum of Fine Arts, Boston, Massachusetts. Courtesy of the Boston Athenaeum.

Charles Willson Peale (1741-1827). The Staircase Group, 1795. (89×39½″)
Philadelphia Museum of Art, Philadelphia, Pennsylvania. George W. Elkins Collection.

traveled to New England where he visited Smibert's studio and met Copley. In 1766 he was sent by a group of Maryland patrons to London, spending three years in West's studio. West and Peale became firm friends, corresponding after Peale's return to America, and years later West sent artistic advice to Peale's sons as they launched their own careers as painters.

Back in America, Peale painted cool, pleasant portraits that reflect the coloristic influence of Joshua Reynolds, the leading portrait painter in London while Peale was there. Although many artists departed from the colonies for Europe on the outbreak of the Revolution, either from loyalist convictions or economic necessity, Peale was an ardent patriot who served in the Continental Army throughout the war. In a memorable 1779 portrait of George Washington (Pennsylvania Academy of Fine Arts, Philadelphia, Pennsylvania), he depicted the victorious general at full length, exaggeratedly attenuated, legs crossed, leaning jauntily against a cannon, with captured Hessian flags representing the Battle of Trenton stacked at his feet and British prisoners from the Battle of Princeton being marched past Nassau Hall in the background. Confidence pervades the portrait, as a relaxed Washington, a smile playing about his lips, with New England, New Jersey and Pennsylvania now cleared of the enemy, seems ready to mount up and ride off to strike another victorious blow elsewhere.

Peale was a man of varied interests, an inveterate tinkerer and inventor, as devoted to science as to art. He established one of the first American museums in Philadelphia in 1786, exhibiting paintings and specimens of natural history cheek by jowl. He was also deeply interested in art instruction, and a leader in the formation of the Columbianum Academy in Philadelphia in 1795, forerunner of the oldest art academy still in existence in America today, the Pennsylvania Academy of Fine Arts, founded in 1807. For the initial exhibition at the Columbianum in 1795, Peale painted *The Staircase Group*, a remarkable double-portrait of two of his sons, Raphaelle and Titian (Peale at this point named his children after artists, including Rembrandt and Angelica Kauffmann; later he named children after scientists, Linnaeus and Franklin). The painting is a "deception." *Trompe l'œil* paintings have enjoyed particular appeal throughout the history of American art. Perhaps this reflects the materialism and pragmatism of American life, its firm commitment to the real world. *The Staircase Group* elicited the same kind of admiration as Copley's portrait of *Thomas Ainslie*, which the sitter's young son had attempted to grasp by the hand. Years later Rembrandt Peale recalled that when President Washington went to see the Columbianum exhibition, *The Staircase Group* caught the corner of his eye. The painting had been intentionally framed in a door jamb and a step had been built out from the base of the picture to the floor, continuing the painted staircase on which the illusion of a dropped ticket of admission to the Columbianum had been painted out into the room itself. As Washington passed the picture, according to Rembrandt, he turned to it and doffed his hat, making a polite little bow to the painted image. The "deception" was a success!

In later years Peale's interest in science overshadowed his interest in art, although he never abandoned the latter completely. In 1806 he painted the fascinating *Exhuming the Mastodon* (Peale Museum, Baltimore, Maryland) which recalled Peale's 1801 expedition to recover dinosaur's bones discovered in a swamp on a New York farm. It shows a large wheel and bucket chain operated by a human treadmill dredging water from the pit in which the bones had been located. Peale's *The Artist in His Museum* of 1822 (Pennsylvania Academy of Fine Arts, Philadelphia, Pennsylvania) is a final monument to a long career, a self-portrait of the artist standing in his museum on the second floor of Independence Hall. His dual interest in art and science is indicated by the juxtaposition of a palette and mastodon bones in the foreground, and echoed in portraits of Revolutionary War heroes, a dinosaur skeleton and various stuffed specimens in the background.

Toward the end of his long and productive career, Peale produced a series of charming landscape views showing scenes around his farm in Germantown. Peale, ever experimental, was dabbling late in life with the kind of artistic expression that was to become dominant in American art in the nineteenth century, paintings of the American landscape.

Asher B. Durand (1796-1886). Kindred Spirits, 1849. (46×36″)
The New York Public Library, New York. Astor, Lenox and Tilden Foundations.

The Search for Identity

IN addition to such familiar obstacles as unsettled political and economic conditions inhibiting patronage of the arts, and the lack of demand for art other than portraiture, American artists in the first half of the nineteenth century faced some new problems. These grew out of two related issues: what kind of art was appropriate for a democracy and what were to be the sources of artistic support in a democracy? Was art *au fond* undemocratic, as John Adams suspected it was, appealing to base primitive instincts, to undemocratic feelings of personal and family pride, to the sensuous rather than the rational nature of man? And from what segment of a democratic society was patronage to come? There was no formal aristocracy, although a *de facto* aristocracy of wealth and political power, especially in Federalist circles, existed. There was no dominant state church to support the arts; indeed Congregationalism and the other large Protestant denominations in America were literally iconoclastic. Moreover the state itself, in contrast to European monarchies, showed little inclination to commission works glorifying the nation and its leaders.

The problems faced by artists in America went beyond rampant philistinism. That could be overcome through education, increased affluence, and the growing awareness that a great nation must achieve world leadership in all areas, including the arts. But assuming adequate support for the arts, what should an American art be? What styles and subjects were appropriate to this unprecedented democracy? The distinctive character of earlier American art had resulted in part from technical inadequacies of the artists, which together with esthetic preference led to emphasis of the surface plane, and in part from the pragmatism of American life, which manifested itself in a taste for realism. Yet the armature on which these national, or rather provincial, characteristics were hung, was European. America was an outpost of European civilization, artistically serviced by itinerant European painters of varying but rarely impressive abilities, and kept at least monochromatically abreast of contemporary developments in European art by means of engravings. After the middle of the eighteenth century American art was further Europeanized by American artists who studied abroad. This dependence on Europe for artists, art ideas and art training had been acceptable in America when it had been a European colony, a place where the synonym for England was "home." It was quite unacceptable in an independent country, determined to stand on its own feet culturally as well as politically. As a result the history of American art during the first seventy-five years of nationhood was in essence a quest for an art expressive of American identity.

Thomas Sully (1783-1872). Lady with a Harp: Eliza Ridgely, 1818. (84⅜×56⅛″)
National Gallery of Art, Washington, D.C. Gift of Maude Monell Vetlesen.

John Neagle (1796-1865). Pat Lyon at the Forge, 1829. (94½×68½″)
Courtesy of the Pennsylvania Academy of the Fine Arts, Philadelphia, Pennsylvania.

Progress, such as it was, came slowly. Portraiture continued to be the primary artistic activity in America during the first half of the nineteenth century. The leading portrait painter in the wake of Gilbert Stuart, following very much in the same tradition of stylish English portraiture, was Thomas Sully (1783-1872). Born in England, Sully was brought to this country before he was ten. He grew up in Charleston, South Carolina and received his first artistic training there. He traveled north in 1807, went to Boston to visit Gilbert Stuart, and finally settled in Philadelphia. A few years later a group of Philadelphia merchants advanced Sully money for a trip to England, to be repaid in copies of old master paintings. In England Sully, like most aspiring American artists, went first to see Benjamin West, a fellow Philadelphian, now over seventy but still active and influential as President of the Royal Academy. Sully, like Stuart earlier, was only interested in painting portraits, and since West had become almost exclusively concerned with historical and religious paintings, he referred Sully to Thomas Lawrence, the leading English portrait painter of the generation after Reynolds and Gainsborough. The strong influence of Lawrence is clearly evident in Sully's full-length portrait of *Eliza Ridgely, the Lady with a Harp.* At his best in idealized portraits of women, Sully, like Lawrence, combines high color and free brushwork to create sleek, occasionally sentimental, prettified images of boneless figures. His portraits of men are somewhat more vigorous, particularly the dramatic portraits of heroes of the War of 1812 painted early in his career, but these are also idealized. Sully's flattering confections earned him great popularity. During his long career he produced about 2600 paintings, almost all of them portraits.

In later years Sully shared his dominance of Philadelphia portraiture with his son-in-law, John Neagle (1796-1865), whose soft, idealizing portraits resemble Sully's. However his masterpiece, a portrait of *Pat Lyon at the Forge,* is strong and impressive. At the time of the portrait Pat Lyon was a large independent-minded man of fifty-seven. In his youth he had been falsely imprisoned on a robbery charge, and after the real culprit was apprehended Lyon had not been immediately released. For some years he lived in poverty and disgrace, resentful of the upper class, whose members he felt had caused his troubles and failed to right the wrong that had been done him. Gifted with a creative intelligence, Lyon the blacksmith eventually became Lyon the wealthy hydraulic engineer, inventor of a successful fire-engine. When he subsequently commissioned this portrait, he specifically wanted to be shown as a smithy at his forge rather than as a gentleman of the class he disdained. Looking the viewer in the eye, Lyon stands by his forge in a leather apron, hammer on anvil, an assistant behind him leaning on the bellows. Through an opening on the left the cupola of Walnut Street Prison is visible, a reminder of Lyon's false imprisonment. This *portrait d'apparat,* a view of a man within the context of his work, hews close to the grain of the American taste for realism in art.

Although many American artists like Sully and Neagle were content to make their living by painting portraits, others struggled against the straight-jacket of limited patronage and, like West and Copley earlier, wanted to try their hand at something more ambitious. As young Samuel F. B. Morse (1791-1872) wrote from England to his father, Jedidiah Morse, minister and author of the first American geography book, a practical man who was opposed to his son's artistic inclinations and skeptical of his ability to make a living as an artist in America by painting anything but portraits: "Had I no higher thoughts than being a first-rate portrait-painter, I would have chosen a far different profession. My ambition is to be among those who shall rival the splendor of the fifteenth century; to rival the genius of a Raphael, a Michael Angelo, or a Titian; my ambition is to be enlisted in the constellation of genius now rising in this country; I wish to shine, not by a light borrowed from them, but to strive to shine the brightest."

After graduating from Yale College, Morse had gone to England in 1811. He studied at the Royal Academy and before returning to America in 1815 painted several history pictures, including *The Dying Hercules* (Yale University Art Gallery, New Haven, Connecticut), a clay model for which won a gold medal for sculpture at the Adelphi Society (only a

plaster cast at the Yale University Art Gallery survives). However, as his father had predicted, Morse found patronage only for portraits on his return to America. Out of necessity he became an itinerant portraitist, spending the winters in Charleston, South Carolina, and working at other times in Boston, New Haven, New York and Washington. A man of many interests, Morse tinkered with inventions (as did the miniature painter, Robert Fulton, inventor of the steamboat); painted large realistic depictions of the interior of the House of Representatives and of the interior of the Louvre which he took on unprofitable traveling exhibitions; led an artistic revolt against the American Academy of Fine Arts in New York, run in a dictatorial manner by aging John Trumbull, becoming first President of the rival National Academy of Design on its founding in 1826; served as first professor of art at New York University; and in 1832 discovered the principles of the telegraph. Morse found his inventions a more promising path to prosperity in this materialistic democracy than his art, and completely abandoned art during the latter half of his life.

John Vanderlyn (1775-1852) resisted the siren song of portraiture more stubbornly than Morse, and in the end experienced much greater frustration. Born in Kingston, New York, Vanderlyn was the grandson of Pieter Vanderlyn, one of the group of artists including the anonymous painter of *John Van Cortlandt* that had worked in the Hudson River Valley early in the eighteenth century. At the age of sixteen Vanderlyn went to New York City, supporting himself by working in an art supply and engraving shop while he studied at one of the earliest academies for art instruction in America, Archibald Robertson's Columbian Academy (not to be confused with Charles Willson Peale's contemporaneous Columbianum Academy in Philadelphia). Gilbert Stuart, a customer at the shop, allowed young Vanderlyn to copy several of his portraits. One of these copies, a portrait of *Aaron Burr*, caught the attention of Burr himself. Burr inquired about the artist, and learned to his dismay that young Vanderlyn had found it necessary to leave New York and return to Kingston for want of support. Moved by the same public spirit that had led Americans of means to send West, Peale, Sully and other aspiring young artists to Europe, Burr undertook to support Vanderlyn financially for as long as might be necessary for him "to cultivate his genius to the highest point of perfection." Burr arranged for Vanderlyn to live and study briefly with Stuart, who had meanwhile moved to Philadelphia, and in the following year, 1796, sent him to Europe. Since Burr's interests lay not in England, where virtually all previous American artists had gone, but France, Vanderlyn became the first major American artist to study in Paris. He enrolled in the studio of André Vincent at the Ecole des Beaux-Arts, where he learned the basic principles of neo-classical art, with its emphasis on drawing and anatomy. Neo-classicism, although it had germinated three decades earlier in the politically potent paintings of Benjamin West, did not come to fruition in England (West as principal painter of history pieces to the king had abandoned in the 1770's impolitic paintings which proclaimed that men could create new and more perfect societies), but in France, where the style was well-suited to the political needs of the French Revolution.

When Vanderlyn returned to America at the turn of the century, Burr advised him to paint a view of Niagara Falls, one of the wonders of the New World, since an engraving of Niagara would find a ready market in Europe. Vanderlyn, determined not to become a portrait painter, accepted the advice. After completing his sketches he returned to Europe in 1803 to arrange for an engraving. He also carried with him a commission from the newly established American Academy of Fine Arts in New York to purchase plaster casts of antique sculpture and copies of old master paintings that could be used for the instruction of young artists. Shortly after his return to Europe Vanderlyn painted *The Death of Jane McCrea* (Wadsworth Atheneum, Hartford, Connecticut) as an illustration for *The Columbiad*, an epic poem written by his American friend in Paris, Joel Barlow. A scene from the time of the American Revolution, the painting shows Indians scalping an American girl. If the behavior of the Indians was not quite what Rousseau had led Europeans to expect from noble savages, the figures themselves were at least based on classical relief sculpture, echoing in a way the analogy between natural and classical man observed by West in his

John Vanderlyn (1775-1852). Marius Amidst the Ruins of Carthage, 1807. (87×68½″)
M. H. de Young Memorial Museum, San Francisco, California. Gift of M. H. de Young.

which exerted a significant and continuing influence upon American colonial painting during the ensuing years. In the painting Berkeley is posed at the right, as if in the act of dictating to the seated figure at the left, Richard Dalton. Berkeley's wife and child and another woman are seated between them. Smibert himself, gazing at the viewer, stands in the extreme left rear next to his nephew, Dr. Thomas Moffatt. Docile as it appears today, the *Bermuda Group*, in the complexity of its formal organization, in its technical competence, and in its convincing realization of solid figures in space was an esthetic bombshell in the art-starved American colonies.

As delays continued to plague the Bermuda expedition (finally abandoned in 1731), Smibert traveled to Boston to survey the art scene. He found a few local artists of limited ability, such as the painter Nathaniel Emmons and Peter Pelham, a mezzotint engraver who had arrived several years earlier from London where Smibert had probably known him. In Boston Smibert exhibited the *Bermuda Group* and several other recent portraits, along with a few of his old master copies. He was warmly welcomed as the prophet of culture to a city in the wilderness. In July 1730 he married wealthy and socially prominent Mary Williams, twenty years his junior, and settled down to spend the rest of his life in snug little Boston. Apparently Smibert found this small provincial capital, similar to the Edinburgh of his youth, a sympathetic milieu for the exercise of his talents. It was much more pleasant to be the best artist in Boston than a painter of the "third rank" in London. Smibert's studio in what later became Scolley Square was in effect the first art museum in America, where the artist not only painted portraits but exhibited them along with the art collection he had brought from Europe.

Despite Smibert's ability and his complete domination of the art scene, Boston did not generate sufficient patronage to enable him to support himself through painting alone. Perhaps this reflected a lingering local anti-image prejudice inherited from the iconoclastic Puritans; perhaps it reflected even more the low priority placed on painting by a pragmatic mercantile society. But Smibert, a provincial Scot, knew how to swim in these waters. He sold art supplies and prints to enlarge his income; he painted portraits that were engraved in mezzotint by Peter Pelham and sold for their mutual profit in Smibert's shop; and he had a wealthy wife. His only lack of success, of which he may not have been aware, was in sustaining the quality of his own work. With the passing of years he relied more and more slavishly on mezzotints for compositional ideas, and faulty drawing increasingly affected adversely the proportions of his figures. During the last years of his life Smibert suffered from failing eyesight. He was forced to give up portraiture, although he continued to divert himself "in a landskip way."

In 1740 twenty-two year old Isaac Royall, who had recently graduated from Harvard, taken a wife, fathered a child, and inherited a substantial estate from his father, a young man on the rise, decided to have a group portrait painted of himself and his young family to celebrate his new eminence. Probably because Smibert at the time was incapacitated by illness, the commission was given to Robert Feke (born 1705/10-after 1750), an artist whose background and career is still shrouded in mystery. Perhaps born and raised in Oyster Bay, Long Island, and perhaps having traveled to Europe in his youth as a mariner, Feke was from the start an artist of considerable sensitivity, particularly as a colorist, despite his apparent lack of professional training. Whether by Feke's design or Royall's orders, the large group portrait of *Isaac Royall and His Family* derives directly from Smibert's *Bermuda Group*. The figures are similarly gathered about a table covered with an oriental carpet. The principal figure stands to the right, holding a book in his right hand. Seated next to him is his young wife, holding an infant, followed to the left by a woman pointing across her body to the left, with landscape and sky in the background. A seated figure at the left end of the table closes the composition.

Compared with the *Bermuda Group*, which Smibert had painted fresh from his career as a competitive portrait painter in London, Feke's early effort seems naive, although hauntingly effective. The color areas float on the surface, and the modeling is not convincing,

John Smibert (1688-1751). Dean George Berkeley and His Party (The Bermuda Group), 1729. (69¾×94½″)
Yale University Art Gallery, New Haven, Connecticut. Gift of Isaac Lathrop of Plymouth, Mass., 1808.

especially the heads of the women and the doll-like child. Whereas Smibert after leaving London became more provincial in America with the passage of time, Feke started out as an untutored provincial and sought increasingly to achieve London standards of sophistication. He too relied on prints, using them as a way of becoming more up to date, choosing those produced by leading contemporary London portraitists such as Thomas Hudson and Joseph Highmore. However, despite his aspiration to be a fashionable portraitist, Feke could never divest his art of the highly developed sense of the surface plane at the expense of solid forms and space that betrays his provincial origin. In Feke's portraits, figures dominate the composition, and the landscape background is little more than a theatrical backdrop, a painted setting. Figures are related to the landscape not by the subtle modeling of solid forms in space but by the interaction of lines in the figure plane with lines in the landscape plane, and by the complementary color play of foreground and background. Despite some stylistic advance in his later work, Feke remained wedded to the two-planar concern with surface design and background that had characterized American art from the start, as in *Mrs. Elizabeth Freake and Daughter Mary*. In Feke's gifted hands this limitation became an asset, not a liability, as he achieved extraordinarily appealing results in color, line and surface design. As a portraitist, Feke was more interested in the decorative possibilities of

comparison of the antique *Apollo Belvedere* with a Mohawk warrior. The composition itself bears a generic resemblance to the Parthenon metopes depicting *The Battle of the Centaurs and the Lapiths.*

In 1805 Vanderlyn went to Rome to study antiquity at first hand. There he painted his most important history picture, *Marius Amidst the Ruins of Carthage.* The painting depicts a defeated Roman general, Caius Marius, seated in front of the ruins of Carthage in a pose borrowed from a classical statue of *Ares,* the god of war (after Scopas). A man who had enjoyed power but now defeated in a civil war and disappointed in his ambition, Marius, his world in ruins about him, meditates revenge. The painting received a gold medal at the Academy Exhibition of 1808 in Paris, and is said to have been admired and selected for the prize by Napoleon, who himself would one day sit on Elba amidst the ruins of his ambition like Marius, and plot his return.

Neo-classical art is humanistic, concerned with what man has accomplished and what he can accomplish. Human actors invariably dominate the scene. *Marius Amidst the Ruins of Carthage* is neo-classical in subject and treatment, although atypical in that no action occurs. Marius is not doing anything; he just sits and broods. The picture cannot simply be read as a story. It requires the active emotional as well as intellectual involvement of the viewer. The viewer must, if he is to approach the essence of the painting, try to imagine what is going on in the mind of Marius. The empathetic participation required of each individual perceiver of the painting is a step beyond Neo-classicism in the direction of Romanticism. Neo-classicism, the artistic arm of the Enlightenment, focused attention on man in society, natural and perfectible, and this led, perhaps unexpectedly but directly, to Romanticism wherein the interest in man in general became interest in individual man, his feelings and emotions rather than his behavior.

Continuing to drift away from pure Neo-classicism, Vanderlyn, on his return to Paris, was less influenced by the classical exercises of his French contemporaries than by the glowing color and subtle chiaroscuro of paintings by Titian and Correggio in the Louvre. Trying his own hand at an original composition in this mode, he painted *Ariadne* (Pennsylvania Academy of Fine Arts, Philadelphia, Pennsylvania), a sensuous representation of ideal female beauty. Ariadne, daughter of Minos, the King of Crete, had fallen in love with Theseus, a prisoner in her father's labyrinth. Unraveling a thread to trace a path to freedom, Ariadne rescued Theseus and they escaped to the idyllic Isle of Naxos. Eventually fickle Theseus became restless and deserted Ariadne. The painting depicts his desertion, nude Ariadne sleeping in the foreground, Theseus sneaking off in the distance.

Vanderlyn wished to return to America, but since he was not a portrait painter, he faced the problem of earning a living. He decided that there was money to be made by combining art and entertainment, exhibiting large panorama paintings to the public. Before leaving France in 1815 he sketched the gardens of Versailles, and when he arrived in America he transferred the sketches to three thousand feet of canvas. He constructed a solid little rotunda in New York where he exhibited this and other panoramas quite successfully. During the winter months he took the panoramas on tour to the South. Within a few years, however, the novelty of the panoramas wore off and public interest withered. Vanderlyn became bitter over the failure of Americans to support art. Toward the end of his life he finally received a commission from Congress to paint *The Landing of Columbus* for the Capitol Rotunda, but his spark was gone. Vanderlyn returned to Paris and with the help of French assistants produced a pedestrian picture. Having failed to find adequate support for his art after his return to America, Vanderlyn never fulfilled his early promise.

During the second half of the eighteenth century the cutting edge of artistic innovation had been a new classicism, the characteristics of which included clarity, order, rationality, a dominance of line over color, sculptural modeling of the human form, an overriding humanistic concern with man, and didacticism. Vanderlyn was the one American artist steeped in French Neo-classicism, but he caught it at ebb tide, and in retrospect appears an anachronism in his own time, although the brooding intensity of Marius seems to catch something of the spirit of the new Romantic movement. If Vanderlyn was artistically *retardataire*, his progressive mirror image was Washington Allston (1779-1843). Born in Charleston, South Carolina, during the American Revolution and named after the national hero, Allston was very much a product of the new generation, eager for fresh experiences. At Harvard he studied the classics but was more profoundly affected by early romantic literature, notably Schiller's *The Robbers* and the gothic novels of Ann Radcliffe, and such melodramatic pictures as Fuseli's illustrations for Boydell's *Shakespeare Gallery*. After his graduation in 1801, Allston and his friend, the Charleston miniature painter, Edward Malbone, sailed for London. Unlike previous American artists who were eager to sit at the feet of Benjamin West, Allston anticipated that West's works, which he knew through prints, would be static, pretentious and dull. He sought more exciting stuff. However when he arrived in London he found to his surprise that West was creating highly romantic pictures, such as *Death on a Pale Horse* (Philadelphia Museum of Art, Philadelphia, Pennsylvania), and soon counted West among his artistic heroes.

Whereas French painting during the last quarter of the eighteenth century had become increasingly neo-classical, painting in England, after an early flirtation in the work of West and others, veered away from Neo-classicism because of its radical political overtones. Subsequent English painting, particularly portraiture, became deeply concerned with color as opposed to the linear stress and muted palette of Neo-classicism, and was strongly influenced by Rubens and by the great Venetian colorists of the sixteenth century. Allston absorbed this in London, and when he went to Paris in 1803 via the Low Countries in the company of Vanderlyn, whom he had met in London, it was not to absorb Neo-classicism but to immerse himself in the art of the past at the Louvre. Copying Rubens, he used a rich glazing technique that perplexed his French contemporaries who were accustomed to flat, opaque surfaces. He studied intently the work of Titian, Tintoretto, and, above all, Veronese, in whose color Allston found an abstract appeal analogous to music. Color, not the events displayed, was for Allston the true subject of Veronese's paintings.

In such early pictures as *Thunderstorm at Sea* (Boston Museum of Fine Arts, Boston, Massachusetts), Allston deployed broad tonal masses of sea and sky, linked closely in hue but with strong contrasts of light and dark, creating a deep space markedly different from the surface immediacy of neo-classical painting. Touches of bright color carry the eye to tiny figures in the pilot boat, and only then does the viewer become aware of the human participants in the dramatic scene. In contrast to neo-classical art, man does not dominate the natural world here; he is at its mercy. The viewer identifies himself with the threatened figures, empathetically experiencing their terror. The participation of each individual perceiver is an essential part of the esthetic experience. The viewer cannot read the picture as a narrative but must become personally involved with it to grasp its meaning.

In 1804-1805 Allston traveled to Rome, making sketches of Swiss scenery on the way, which he subsequently combined into imaginative landscapes, such as *Diana in the Chase* (Fogg Art Museum, Harvard University, Cambridge, Massachusetts). These paintings, built up of washes of translucent glaze which successively modify the color beneath, are reveries on the timeless grandeur and beauty of nature, on the endless cycle of life and death in the natural landscape.

Allston returned to Boston in 1808, but rather than paint portraits for a living, he went back to England several years later. Settling in London, he painted highly imaginative subjects such as *The Dead Man Revived by Touching the Bones of the Prophet Elisha* (Pennsylvania Academy of Fine Arts, Philadelphia, Pennsylvania), with its complex interplay of gesture and expression as the human actors become aware of and respond variously to the miracle that occurs.

Allston went to Paris again in 1817, and was once more enchanted by the Venetian paintings at the Louvre. *Elijah in the Desert*, painted shortly afterwards, reflects his renewed interest in color. It strikes a harmonious chord of warm brown earth and cool blue mountains and sky. The small, solitary figure of Elijah kneels in the foreground, a dead tree

Washington Allston (1779-1843). Elijah in the Desert fed by the Ravens, 1818. (43¾×72½″)
Courtesy, Museum of Fine Arts, Boston, Massachusetts. Gift of Mrs. Samuel and Miss Alice Hooper.

towering above him. As opposed to Vanderlyn's neo-classical paintings in which foreground figures dominate the composition, the figure here is dominated by the landscape. The brown earth is sere. Dry stones and dead trees predominate over a few foliate elements to the left. It is a realm of death, not life. Yet the cool, distant sky and mountainscape seem to hold forth a promise of spiritual refreshment. The starving prophet kneels in the barren desert and prays, reaching out to the world of the spirit which lies beyond. The blue of his robe, echoing the color of mountains and sky, implies his identification with the spiritual world. His prayers have been heard and answered; the ravens, normally scavengers who would pick his dead bones clean, fly down to deliver life-giving bread.

The huge *Belshazzar's Feast* (Detroit Institute of Arts, Detroit, Michigan), a "sublime" conception, very different in character from the dreamy *Elijah*, was almost complete when Allston returned permanently to the United States in 1818. He hoped to finish the picture promptly, but found it financially expedient to paint a number of small pictures for immediate sale. To alleviate this necessity and allow Allston to devote himself uninterruptedly to his master work, a group of Bostonians formed a trust and put up ten thousand dollars to buy the picture in advance. This generous patronage, unprecedented in America, unhappily became an albatross around Allston's neck. Accepting Gilbert Stuart's advice to change the perspective in the picture, Allston undertook extensive and time-consuming alterations to please his patrons. By this time, his esthetic interests had progressed from "sublimity" to a completely different kind of painting, tranquil and meditative. Yet he was trapped by his obligation to complete *Belshazzar*. He kept at it, painting and repainting, sometimes rolling up the canvas and putting it away for awhile, but always returning, working on it to the very day of his death. A humiliation to the artist and an embarrassment to the good citizens of Boston who had tried to be helpful, the painting became such a sore subject that friends of the gentle Allston could not mention the picture in his presence.

Whereas most creative artists in America suffered from neglect and lack of support, Allston's creative spark had been smothered by an excess of helpfulness. The "Allston Trust" failed in its purpose, but it was a hopeful indication of the potential for art patronage in America. Wealthy Americans had in the past assisted young artists by subsidizing European travel and study, and, in the nineteenth century, became active in organizing academies such as the American Academy of Fine Arts in New York (1803) and the Pennsylvania Academy of Fine Arts in Philadelphia (1807) where artists could receive instruction in this country. However support of art and artists was not effectively continued to the essential final step, the purchase of pictures. American collectors of art, few in number at best, preferred European works, old and new; they did not "collect" American art. American paintings as a rule entered American collections only incidentally, as when portraits of the collector or members of his family were commissioned. However by the end of the eighteenth century a small market for topographical landscapes, that is for portraits of places, began to develop.

Throughout most of the seventeenth and eighteenth centuries the American landscape had been considered a source of danger, a sheltering darkness from whence came Indian attacks, an inconvenient wilderness that blocked the way from place to place and that had to be obliterated to create fields and meadowlands. Although the wilderness supplied wood for building and fuel, essential for life support in the New World, it was to be conquered and used rather than admired. John Smibert spoke of painting some landscapes at the end of his life, when failing eyesight ended his career as a portrait painter, but by and large landscape painting was virtually non-existent in America until the last decade of the eighteenth century. A small group of minor English landscapists, the most important of whom was Francis Guy (1760-1820), came to America and painted views of gentlemen's estates in Maryland and Northern Virginia. The most ambitious early landscape was the large *Landscape: Looking East from Denny Hill* (Worcester Art Museum, Worcester, Massachusetts), a prospect painted in the 1790's by the Connecticut portrait painter Ralph Earl as a remembrance for a patron who was moving from his lifetime home. At the turn of the century William Birch (1755-1834) and his son Thomas (1779-1851) made numerous topographical views of Philadelphia for publication. By the 1820's increasing interest in the American landscape for its own sake surfaced in the works of Thomas Doughty (1793-1856), perhaps America's first real landscape painter. A sportsman who loved to hunt and fish, Doughty painted quiescent and somewhat stylized views that record his personal affection for nature. Another early landscapist, Asher B. Durand (1796-1886), began as a highly skilled engraver (his reputation was greatly enhanced by a successful engraving of John Vanderlyn's *Ariadne*, which he owned). Active in New York artistic life, Durand was a founding member and second president of the National Academy of Design.

In 1825 three landscapes of unusual quality appeared in a shop window in New York. Durand bought one, as did John Trumbull, president of the American Academy of Fine Arts, and William Dunlap, painter, theatrical producer, and in 1832 author of the earliest book on American art, *The History of the Rise and Progress of the Arts of Design in the United States*. These three landscapes, recognized immediately as remarkable works by the most knowing eyes in New York, were painted by Thomas Cole (1801-1848). Cole had come to New York from Ohio, where he had gone with his family as a boy of seventeen after their arrival in America from England. In New York Cole quickly established himself as America's leading landscape painter. During the good weather he would travel throughout New England and along the Hudson River, making drawings and oil sketches which he

worked up into finished canvases during the winter in his studio. Soon a whole throng of artists, popularly known as the Hudson River School, literally followed in Cole's footsteps.

Cole and Allston stand as the two major American painters of the first half of the nineteenth century. Their eminence results not so much from their mastery of the craft of painting, although this they had, as from the powers of mind which they brought to their art. Author of a treatise on art theory entitled *Lectures on Art*, of a number of poems including the substantial *Sylphs of the Seasons*, and of *Monaldi*, a gothic romance, Allston was the intimate friend of major literary figures in England and America, notably Samuel Taylor Coleridge and Washington Irving. Cole's literary and philosophical counterpart was the poet William Cullen Bryant. The parallel between Cole as painter and Bryant as poet, particularly in their sensitive response to nature, was fully appreciated in their own day. In commemoration of Cole's death Durand painted *Kindred Spirits* depicting Cole and Bryant on a rocky ledge in a picturesque forest setting.

Cole went to Europe in 1829 for three years of intensive study. He was particularly interested in the work of the great seventeenth century landscapist, Claude Lorrain. Among moderns he was most profoundly influenced by J. M. W. Turner, another Claudian, and John Martin, whose visionary art struck a responsive chord with Cole's similar taste for melodrama on a gargantuan scale.

Cole was greatly affected by the surviving ruins of classical antiquity in Italy, not for the moral and social lessons that earlier generations had found there, but in themselves as mute testimonials to the impermanence of the human condition, to the inescapable fact that life is change, that everything rises and falls, lives and dies; as reminders of the transience of one's own moment in time. Ruins also suggested to Cole that the surface appearance of a place is deceptive, affording only a slight clue to the historical richness of all that had transpired there. The roll of years over a site left behind deep substrata of history, out of which the artist's imagination could dredge the secrets of the past. Two early paintings representing a scene from James Fenimore Cooper's 1826 novel, *The Last of the Mohicans* (Wadsworth Atheneum, Hartford, Connecticut; New York State Historical Association, Cooperstown, New York), reveal Cole's predisposition for this type of thinking, depicting the event as a transient flicker in the timelessness of a mountain landscape. The *Titan's Goblet* (Metropolitan Museum of Art, New York), painted just after Cole's return from Europe, deals with the theme of time and place in a bizarre vision. A gigantic drinking vessel rests on the surface of the earth, its rim enclosing a lake so lofty that it touches the clouds. Along the rim of the goblet, a civilization thrives, its ships scuttling back and forth across the lake. Lacking a true perspective on themselves, the people who live in this place are presumably unaware that their physical environment is not a natural part of the landscape, but rather the result of some incredible titanic event.

As Cole rambled in Italy amidst ruins surviving from ancient civilizations that had played out their brief dramas on the permanent stage of the natural landscape, contemplating time, change and the transience of civilizations as artistic themes, he began to think in terms of series of paintings rather than single canvases. The result was *The Course of Empire* painted on his return from Italy for his New York patron, Luman Reed. The series consists of five large canvases, each depicting the same scene, although the viewpoint shifts. In the first painting, *The Savage State*, a storm moves off to the left and the break of day reveals the dawn of civilization under a clear sky. Man, the hunter, tracks his prey in a wild and uncivilized landscape. The second picture, *The Pastoral State*, represents an idyllic arcadian scene under a fresh mid-morning sun. Simple roads traverse the hunter's former path. Wild animals have been replaced by domestic herds of sheep guarded by their shepherd. An old man draws geometric patterns in the dust with a stick, suggestive of the beginnings of mathematics and science. Ships traverse the lagoon, as commerce springs forth. In the distance a temple with monolithic stone columns suggests an emergent spiritual nature and the growth of religion. The third painting presents *The Triumph of Empire*. The scene has now shifted to the shores of the lagoon. A horned mountain on the right, which had

Thomas Cole (1801-1848). The Course of Empire: The Savage State, 1833-1836. (39¼×63¼")
The New-York Historical Society, New York.

appeared in the distance in the earlier views, guards one entrance to the harbor. A lighthouse stands on the other side. A noonday sun pours down on a fantastic architectural complex, a great white city like the imaginative views of Dido's Carthage painted by Turner and Claude. In the fourth scene, *The Destruction of Empire*, the point of view retreats to the head of the lagoon, exposing a panoramic view of unchecked carnage and destruction, perhaps inspired by John Martin's *Fall of Babylon*. The time is late afternoon. A sublime stormy sky provides an appropriate backdrop for the turbulent scene below. In the fifth and concluding scene, *The Desolation of Empire*, the viewpoint retreats still further. Beneath a calm moonlit sky, growth-covered ruins of the expired civilization moulder back into the earth. Only the great natural forms, the mountain and the lagoon, persist. Yet the implication is that all is not ended. After a stormy night to complete the ruin, dawn will bring a new life, a fresh savage state, and the cycle will be repeated, raising up a new civilization unaware that all of this had transpired before. Only the mountain and the lagoon will share the secret.

The essence of what Cole said melodramatically in *The Course of Empire* is distilled in his best single natural landscapes, such as *Schroon Mountain*. Slanting trees enframe a panoramic opening that draws the viewer as if he were a disembodied spirit down into the valley where the river flows, then around to the right beyond the foreground mountain to a widening of the river, perhaps a lake, and then up the slope to the mountain peak that dominates the composition, its point piercing through the clouds to a clear blue opening in a stormy skyscape. No living being is seen, yet the picture throbs with life. One of the two

prominent trees in the left foreground is alive while the other is dead and blasted, a skeletal thing; the tree on the right has both living and dead limbs. These tree forms, their limbs extended like arms, stand in the natural landscape as human surrogates. Their fate is man's fate. The landscape is decked with autumn foliage, its fiery beauty a prelude to death. But beneath the death is life. All is change, process, flux. A great civilization may have flourished on this very spot, or perhaps someday will, but for the moment the life cycles of unspoiled nature pulse regularly, the sky fills with storm and clears, day is replaced by night which is replaced by day, the river flows, and the mountains endure. Like Bryant in *Thanatopsis*, Cole saw the physical world as the handiwork of God and pervaded by Him. It is a glorious tomb, where dead heroes dwell and where we and our children and our children's children will join them in the bosom of the Divine Spirit. This is what Durand implies, a little stiffly, by the juxtaposition of Cole and Bryant in *Kindred Spirits*, and what Cole actually achieves in *Schroon Mountain*, a painting palpitating with life force and infused with Divine immanence.

Another of Cole's series is *The Voyage of Life* of 1839. In the first of four scenes, *Childhood*, a small boat with a golden figurehead, bearing a child and his guardian angel, issues from the circular opening of a dark cave (a remarkable pre-Freudian image). In one of Cole's early landscapes, *The Expulsion from the Garden of Eden* of 1827 (Boston Museum of Fine Arts, Boston, Massachusetts), the tiny figures of Adam and Eve depart fearfully from a sunny paradise to enter a dark, terrifying craggy landscape. In terms of romantic art theory they were moving from the Beautiful to the Sublime. In *Childhood* the situation of Adam

Thomas Cole (1801-1848). Schroon Mountain, the Adirondacks, 1833. (39⅜×63″)
Cleveland Museum of Art, Cleveland, Ohio. Hinman B. Hurlbut Collection.

and Eve is reversed; the figures come out of the "sublime" unknown to enter the "beautiful" natural world. In *Youth* the young man in his boat sets out from the shore, reaching toward a vision of the heavenly kingdom. His guardian angel bids him farewell. The boat is tossed about in *Manhood,* a storm-filled scene, shooting past rock-spiked rapids and yawning chasms. The young man stands calmly in his boat, his hands clasped in prayer, trusting to divine guidance. In *Old Age* all is again placid. An old man sits in his boat, the figurehead worn down to a burnished nub. The angel flies ahead to lead the way across calm waters to the reward that lies beyond. The voyage is almost ended.

Thomas Cole brought new respectability to a previously neglected branch of American painting, landscape, demonstrating that it could incorporate philosophical and religious content worthy of the attention of artists and the support of patrons. Nationalistic pride also stimulated the domestic market for these works. Spurred by Cole's achievement, many younger artists turned to the American landscape as an appropriate subject. And when interest in New England and Hudson River landscapes inevitably began to pall, westward expansion opened new vistas to paint. The interest of Americans in the western territories was intensified by a sense of "Manifest Destiny," a belief that divine will coincided with national interest in the American push to the Pacific. This worked to the advantage of Albert Bierstadt (1830-1902), an artist of the West who achieved great popularity during the third quarter of the century. Bierstadt traveled extensively through the Rocky Mountains and Northern California, making drawings and oil sketches on paper from which he painted enormous canvases on his return. Paintings such as the *Rocky Mountains* (Metropolitan Museum of Art, New York) and *Mount Corcoran* (Corcoran Gallery of Art, Washington, D. C.) dwarfed most Hudson River canvases and effectively conveyed a sense of the magnitude of the western landscape to awed Eastern viewers. Even such delightful small canvases as *Lake Tahoe* have an inherent monumentality, suggestive of the grand scale of the West. Although Bierstadt did not use his art as a forum to express his views, he clearly expressed a sense of the unspoiled perfection of the West as it stood. When Indians are shown, as in *Rocky Mountains*, they, like the deer, bear and other forms of animal life depicted, exist in harmony with the magnificent natural setting. There is an obvious implication that the coming of the white man will change all of this, and the viewer frequently is aware of playing the role of an intruder, an interloper in a natural paradise.

Last of the Buffalo (Corcoran Gallery of Art, Washington, D.C.) is a memorable image of a dramatic clash between Indians and buffalo on the prairie. For centuries the Indian had relied upon the buffalo for food, shelter, and clothing, hunting him relentlessly. In the painting, a mounted Indian drives his spear deep into a buffalo, who glares with reddened eye and lowers his horns to charge with a ferocity born of desperation. Around these ancient adversaries locked in combat lie the dead and dying, Indians and buffalo. This tragic encounter will be their last, as the coming of the white man dooms them both.

Although Bierstadt stands in the same dominant position in relation to Western landscape as Cole in the East, he was not really Cole's artistic kinsman. A native of Germany who later returned to Düsseldorf for four years of art study, Bierstadt reflects a more sentimental and less metaphysical tradition. Cole's one major direct descendant was Frederick Edwin Church (1826-1900), his only pupil during the last few years of his life. Church's earliest New England landscapes continue the type of panoramic outlook that Cole was developing in his own late work. His subsequent dramatic canvases painted in far-flung corners of the globe rival Bierstadt's in scale, but their philosophical content comes directly from Cole. Church carried Cole's concern with the ebb and flow of history over a fixed site in the natural landscape back a step further to the history of the landscape itself. Much influenced by Alexander von Humboldt's *Cosmos* (1847), he combined a scientific interest in geology and the history of the earth with a theological belief that the best avenue for an approach to God could be found through the most dramatic natural phenomena of the earth itself. If God made the earth and is immanent in it, then certainly He reveals Himself most clearly in the earth's most spectacular and awesome displays. Church's monu-

Albert Bierstadt (1830-1902). Lake Tahoe, 1868. (13×16⅛″)
Courtesy of the Fogg Art Museum, Harvard University, Cambridge, Massachusetts. Gift of Mr. and Mrs. Frederic H. Curtiss.

mental canvases frequently contain Christian references, whether overt, as in the shrine in *The Heart of the Andes* (Metropolitan Museum of Art, New York) of 1859, or implied, as in the cruciform golden reflections of the sun on the surface of a crimson lake in the several views of *Cotopaxi*.

Church traveled all over the world in search of dramatic subject matter, to South America, Labrador, Europe and the Near East, but he also found it close at home. He made his early reputation in 1857 with *Niagara* (Corcoran Gallery of Art, Washington, D.C.). Church believed Niagara Falls to be meaningfully symbolic in nationalistic terms for America. If one were closest to God in the most dramatic parts of nature, surely Niagara Falls was an American blessing. God's immanence in natural phenomena implied presence, which by extension implied divine favor on the place or country in which the phenomenon was located. For a country caught up in the full flood of western expansion, imbued with nationalistic fervor and convinced of "Manifest Destiny," the evidence that God was on our side was undoubtedly popular. Church carried his chauvinism to a mawkish extreme in a

Frederick E. Church (1826-1900). Twilight in the Wilderness, 1860. (40×64″)
Cleveland Museum of Art, Cleveland, Ohio. Mr. and Mrs. William H. Marlatt Fund.

chromolithograph, *Our Banner in the Sky.* It depicted a star-studded blue firmament and bars of white cloud in a sunset sky streaked with red, beyond a bare tree on which an eagle perched, creating an incredible natural simulation of a fluttering American flag. Published shortly after the outbreak of the Civil War, the message of the picture was clear; God stood with the Union.

In *Niagara* a rainbow is formed by the spray from the Falls. Often used in symbolic connection with the New World, the rainbow represents promise, a fresh start, which was what the New World was all about. As a natural spectrum, the rainbow also exercised for Church the same kind of scientific appeal coupled with symbolism as did dramatic geological phenomena. Another symbol for a new start in the New World was Adam; the American was Adam, a new man. In the symbol-infused landscapes of Church, large trees in the foreground, rooted in the American soil, their leafy arms twisting in space, stand as man's proxy in the natural landscape, as new men in the New World. Nowhere is this symbolism more overt or more moving than in Church's thundering *Twilight in the Wilderness.* Fiery red clouds surge across the sky in bold diagonal rhythms. Nature is the manifestation of God, and here divine purpose moves in echo of the westward movement of Manifest Destiny. A purple mountain crowns the composition in the distance, at the end of the flowing carmine river. The trees stand like sentinels; they are us and we are they, surveying this vast and moving new world landscape that belongs to us, Americans, the new men.

Church's combined interest in art and the earth sciences places him partly within one of the most venerable traditions in America, that of the artist-naturalist. From the time of the earliest explorations, artists had depicted the natural phenomena of America, often in engravings published for broader distribution to Europeans curious about the strange flora and fauna of the New World. More than with most other categories of artists, the artist-naturalist made pictures with an eye toward publication. Early practitioners, such as Mark Catesby (1679?-1749), William Bartram (1739-1823) and Alexander Wilson (1766-1813), traveled extensively throughout eastern North America, plunging into unspoiled areas, recording their observations in pictures and publishing the results on their return to civilization. The artist-naturalist is the counterpart of the artist-inventor in his scientific curiosity about the real world. The archetypal figure in American art was Charles Willson Peale, who was both artist-inventor and artist-naturalist. One of his sons, the second Titian Ramsey Peale (born after the death of the lad with the same name who appears at the top of the steps in *The Staircase Group*) was an artist-naturalist who sailed on several voyages of geographical exploration to the South Pacific.

The most justly famed of all American artist-naturalists is John James Audubon (1785-1851). Born in Haiti of French parents and educated in France, he came to the United States in 1804. He returned briefly to France in 1805-1806. At one point Audubon studied drawing with Jacques-Louis David, and if he is to be fitted into any artistic tradition, it is French Neo-Classicism. However Audubon defies categorization by the originality of his creative power. He traveled extensively, recording the birds and later the mammals of North America. Rendering the various species in beautiful drawings and watercolors, Audubon was not satisfied with accuracy of surface description. He sought to capture the character as well as the external appearance of each living thing. Brilliantly introducing sparse but graphic settings suggestive of the habits of each creature, he would indicate the ferocity of a predator by showing it with a small creature clutched in its bloody claws, or the nocturnal habits of an owl by depicting it wide-eyed on a branch while all else drowses along a moonlit river, or the world of the turkey cock by observing him from his own eye level, providing a turkey's-eye view of the world. Audubon possessed an almost oriental interest in the essence of things, and like a Chinese painter he disposed his forms, notably in such watercolors as *Purple Grackle*, with a precise and perfect sense of design, achieving balance, or sedate movement, or nervous agitation, or whatever the character of the subject required.

Martin Johnson Heade (1814-1904) combines aspects of both Audubon and Church in his art. Like Audubon he was so attentive to nature that he is in some regards as much a naturalist as an artist. Like Church, he traveled to South America, although not to paint the dramatic Andes. Heade painted innumerable intimate studies of the flora and fauna of the rain forests of Brazil, such as the exquisite *Orchids, Passion Flowers and Hummingbird* intended as an illustration for a projected but never completed book on the hummingbirds of South America. Heade also worked in Florida, where the tropical conditions appealed to him. However he most frequently chose as subject matter the marshlands of New England and New Jersey. Although marshes are less familiar as a subject for art than the sea, the mountains or the forest, Heade knew the marshes as a dramatic and enchanting part of the world, quickened by animal, bird and insect life; by moving patterns of land, grass and water; and above all by their dramatic response to light, especially at dawn and dusk. Heade's long horizontal marsh scenes present a panorama of swiftly changing atmospheric effects. Heade shared with Bierstadt and Church, more evident in the latter two's delightful small oils and sketches based on direct observation of nature than in their large canvases, a strong interest in the transitory effects of nature—the appearance of clouds, the visual effect of light filtering down upon the landscape under varying atmospheric conditions, the approach of a storm, the fleeting brilliance of the sunset. Indeed many landscape painters in the third quarter of the century had this concern, and produced some of the most beautiful American landscapes. Unaccountably neglected until recent times, these artists included second generation Hudson River School figures like John F. Kensett (1818-1872); highly individualistic painters such as Fitz Hugh Lane (1804-1865), overlooked like Heade until recently, a master of the effects of light on water; and sophisticated artists like Sanford R. Gifford (1823-1880) who was aware of the atmospheric innovations of Turner in England,

Martin Johnson Heade (1819-1904). Orchids, Passion Flowers and Hummingbird, 1880. (20×14″)
Collection of Mr. and Mrs. Robert C. Graham, New York.

John James Audubon (1785-1851). Purple Grackle, 1822. Watercolor. (23⅞×18½″)
The New-York Historical Society, New York.

and pioneered a peculiarly American movement known as Luminism. Contemporaneous with Impressionism in France, American Luminism was less adventurous coloristically, never breaking the palette into dabs of pure color. Luminist canvases are gentle, often suffused with a golden glow as sunlight pervades a mist-filled atmosphere.

Whereas for Cole nature had been the constant against which the parade of civilizations and the passing life of man provided change, for Heade and his contemporaries the observer is constant, and nature is in flux, ever shifting in its moods and appearance. Heade's mastery of the transient effects of nature is evident in his tender landscape, *Spring Shower*,

Attributed to Ammi Phillips (1788-1865). Portrait of Harriet Leavens. (56¼×27″)
Courtesy of the Fogg Art Museum, Harvard University, Cambridge, Massachusetts. Gift, Estate of Harriet Anna Niel.

breath propels sailing ships over the water. Waves pulsating with the life force of the sea move rhythmically toward the shore until they are stopped by an abrupt cliff. The incessant sea laps at the immovable shore, and between these forces, amidst stones and rocks and dead branches that are mute testimony to past conflicts between sea and land, a small, perishable human ponders the meaning of it all.

Perhaps the best known of all American folk painters is Edward Hicks (1780-1849). An active Pennsylvania Quaker, Hicks devoted much of his art to the service of his faith. He took the general theme of William Penn's "Holy Experiment," painted much earlier by another Quaker artist from Pennsylvania, Benjamin West, and explored it in a series of memorable representations of the *Peaceable Kingdom*. These invariably depict a menagerie of beasts lying down in peace and harmony with a child in their midst, often in combination with a river landscape and the scene of William Penn receiving the charter for the colony of Pennsylvania or the scene of Penn's treaty with the Indians, reproduced from West's painting. Hicks belonged to the professional or artisan end of the folk art scale, having been apprenticed to a coachmaker, for seven years painting decorative panels, and later he carried on the craft as a painter of tavern and shop signs. Among his most handsome works are several farm scenes, such as *The Residence of David Twining*, a delightful echo of the early tradition of plantation views. The gathering of animals in the left foreground is reminiscent of a *Peaceable Kingdom*, and indeed this is a peaceable kingdom, albeit domestic rather than social or theological. The fruits of industry and domestic harmony are evident in the prosperity and tranquility enjoyed by this Quaker family in America.

Am. 35

William Sidney Mount (1807-1868). The Painter's Triumph, 1838. (19½×23½")
Courtesy of the Pennsylvania Academy of the Fine Arts, Philadelphia, Pennsylvania.

Art for the People

THE turn to the American landscape in the nineteenth century constituted a major step toward the development of an essentially American art. However for most artists landscape painting did not resolve the problem of insufficient patronage. With such notable exceptions as John Vanderlyn's panoramas and the large canvases of Church and Bierstadt, specifically produced for public exhibition, the taste for landscape was limited to a restricted circle of collectors and connoisseurs.

Widespread support in the nineteenth century was gained not by depictions of the American landscape, but of American life. Genre painting, the representation of scenes of everyday human activity, was the natural counterpart to landscape painting in that both were concerned with the world as it is. An art for and about people, genre painting became literally popular in America simultaneously with the rise of Jacksonian democracy. In so doing, it resolved the problem of artistic support and the development of an appropriate art for a democracy.

William Sidney Mount's *The Painter's Triumph* explains the success of genre painting. The scene represents the interior of an artist's studio. Color, except in the costumes, is muted. Details are carefully drawn. The floorboards converging on the far wall provide a perspective setting for the careful placement of objects, creating a convincing illusion of real space. The broad flow of light from the front right casts shadows that further define and locate physical objects. It seems to enter through much of the wall, suggesting that the studio is a small converted barn with an open sliding door, such as Mount often used as the setting for his genre scenes. The studio is sparsely furnished. Two figures, an artist and a rustic visitor, face a painting on an easel. The artist points to the canvas with his right hand, at the same time brandishing his brushes and palette aloft in a fencer's pose, as if elated that through the brilliance of his brushwork he had scored a touch. The visitor leans forward, resting his hands on his knees, and examines the painting. His clothing and buggy whip suggest that he is a local farmer or teamster, rather than a knowing connoisseur, who has stopped in to visit his friend, the artist, in his barn-studio. As he studies the picture, particularly that portion toward which the artist points, his face creases in a smile. Since the painting elicits a spontaneous response from the unsophisticated visitor, it must obviously be readily comprehensible. Like *The Painter's Triumph* itself, the painting must represent something familiar, some aspect of the real world in realistic terms.

An appreciation of realism in art is the most widespread and the least sophisticated of all the criteria of excellence. It is, indeed, the lowest common denominator of artistic taste.

Admiration is elicited by the artist's technical ingenuity, his wizardry with the brush, in achieving realistic pictorial effects that rival reality itself. Art that permits the viewer to recognize what he knows in life, that evokes admiration for the artist's skill at replication, requires no special training or skill to comprehend. Through it the artist can communicate directly with the ordinary public, as in *The Painter's Triumph*. In America the potential public for this sort of art was considerable. The penchant for realism, deeply rooted in the American character, reflecting a pragmatic and materialistic value system, has already been noted.

As in *The Painter's Triumph*, genre paintings often tell some kind of simple story, and the viewer simply reads the picture in literary terms. Indeed genre scenes often were illustrations taken from literature rather than life. Painters found increasing artistic inspiration in American literature as it flowered in the nineteenth century. The dramatic narratives of James Fenimore Cooper and the richly textured stories of Washington Irving inspired artists like John Quidor (1801-1881), just as the poetry of William Cullen Bryant inspired Thomas Cole. Born in Tappan, New York, a small village that still bore the imprint of its early days as a Dutch settlement, Quidor studied art in New York City with the portrait painter, John Wesley Jarvis. However when he launched out on his own, it was as a painter of literary illustrations rather than portraits. Quidor differed from most literary illustrators in that his pictures were not intended to accompany published editions of literary works. The written words simply provided him with the inspiration for the visual recreation of a scene. Each picture is inevitably literary, meant to be read like a story, and its effectiveness hinges on its success in communicating that story. Formal characteristics serve not their own ends but the ends of the plot.

In Quidor's *The Money Diggers*, a scene taken from Washington Irving's *Tales of a Traveller*, Wolfert Webber, with the aid of the nefarious Dr. Knipperhausen, attempts to retrieve a hoard of buried pirate gold. Just as the digging uncovers a treasure chest, the ghost of the drowned buccaneer, "grinning hideously," rises over a rocky embankment behind them. Sam the Negro scampers out of the hole in terror; Dr. Knipperhausen's knees knock together in fear at this unexpected development and he begins to pray in German; Wolfert, in surprise and horror, raises his arms to ward off the apparition. The frantic movements of the figures are echoed by the expressive and tortured gestures of the branches on the trees around them. The scene is dramatically lit by firelight, with secondary illumination from Wolfert's forgotten lantern in the foreground and the ghostly moon that rises behind the embankment. Color, used sparingly in the flames, Wolfert's cape, Sam's vest, and the pirate's cap, effectively leads the eye through the composition. The picture amusingly conveys comic confusion and the cowardice of these inept villains caught out in their wickedness.

The most effective and important genre paintings in the nineteenth century, whether humorous or serious, were derived from actual aspects of American life. The two major artists in this vein were William Sidney Mount (1807-1868) in the East and George Caleb Bingham (1811-1879) in the West. William Sidney Mount was born and raised on Long Island, not far from New York City. He entered the school of the National Academy of Design during its first year, 1826. Although he admired history painting and made some early efforts in that direction, he soon recognized that his peculiar gift was for "comic pictures." He was advised to study the work of the Dutch seventeenth century masters of everyday life, especially Jan Steen. When his period of study was ended, Mount moved back to his beloved rural Long Island where he spent the remainder of his life. However he remained active in the affairs of the National Academy of Design, and exhibited there annually until his death. Despite constant offers from New York patrons and dealers to send him abroad, Mount always demurred, saying "I am contented to remain a while longer in our own great country."

Mount was a slow and painstaking artist, and his production was limited. However his work became widely known through engravings and lithographs. Prints enabled Mount to tap that broad popular market which was the potential source of extensive patronage in democratic America. Mount consciously directed his art toward the esthetic level of his audience. His artistic dictum was "paint pictures that will take with the public—never paint for the few, but for the many." His goal may not have been lofty, but it was appropriate to America in the nineteenth century.

Another important but short-lived means by which American artists reached a broad public was the American Art Union. Organized in 1838 as the Apollo Association, the Art Union used membership fees to publish a news letter, to distribute to each member an engraving of a work by a distinguished American artist or an illustrated book, and to purchase a number of paintings which were distributed by lot at the annual meeting. The Art Union thus became an important source of patronage, with a pool of cash available each year for the purchase of representative works by American artists. This assured patronage fostered interest in art as a viable career, and a noticeable increase in the number of young Americans becoming artists paralleled the life-span of the Art Union. Through the lottery, American paintings were distributed to lucky winners throughout the country. Although this seemed an ideal way for art to achieve broadly based popular support appropriate for a democracy and to develop a wider interest in art, moral scruples about lotteries led to legislation that closed down the Art Union in the early 1850's. One result was financial hardship for artists who lost a dependable source of patronage.

John Quidor (1801-1881). The Money Diggers, 1832. (16¾×21½")

The Brooklyn Museum, Brooklyn, New York. Gift of Mr. and Mrs. A. Bradley Martin, 1948.

Mount was sufficiently popular not to suffer greatly from the demise of the Art Union. He had many important patrons who were happy to have his work. *Eel Spearing at Setauket*, painted in 1845 for a wealthy New Yorker, George Washington Strong, reflected the stylistic lessons Mount had learned from Dutch genre painting of the seventeenth century. The color is restrained, as in *The Painter's Triumph*. The pervasive sepia monochrome avoids strong coloristic assertion of the picture plane and permits a more realistic illusion of solid forms in space. The picture is a rural echo of Copley's *Watson and the Shark* with a Negro as a main character, a spear about to be thrust into the water, and a dominant triangular composition. However the modest artistic intent here is quite different. There are no aspirations toward history painting, no echoes of the *Borghese Warrior*, no striking innovations in dress or setting. The young boy and the Negro woman are on an eel-catching excursion. The day is clear, the water calm, the landscape tranquil. The task at hand is simply an excuse for a delightful outing, more sport than work, as the picnic basket and the pet dog in the boat further suggest. However at the moment everything is concentrated on the business at hand. The boy uses his oar as a rudder to steady the boat on its slow course. He and the dog are motionless. The woman stares down and ahead, focussing the entire composition on the unseen target.

Mount frequently used a Negro as a central figure, and invariably the Negro is presented sympathetically, never caricatured or lampooned. Quite often the Negro appears in conjunction with music. In *The Power of Music* (1847, The Century Association, New York)

William Sidney Mount (1807-1868). Eel Spearing at Setauket, 1845. (29×36″)
New York State Historical Association, Cooperstown, New York.

George Caleb Bingham (1811-1879). Fur Traders Descending the Missouri, about 1845. (29×36½″)
The Metropolitan Museum of Art, New York. Jesup Fund, 1933.

a handsome Negro leans against the door of a barn, separated from the fiddler and his
audience within, yet rapt by the music and, like the thoughtful Indian in West's *Death of
Wolfe,* apparently more in tune with the essence of the moment than the active participants.

George Caleb Bingham, who depicted life along the Mississippi River, Mark Twain's
world of Huckleberry Finn and Tom Sawyer, was Mount's Western counterpart. Bingham
grew up in Franklin, Missouri, on the banks of the Mississippi. Self-taught, he began his
career as an itinerant portrait painter. His early portraits are quite primitive, but in the late
1830's he worked in Philadelphia and his style grew more sophisticated under the influence
of Sully and Neagle. Simultaneously he began to paint genre scenes depicting the life of
boatmen on the Mississippi River which attracted interest when they were exhibited at the
National Academy of Design. In the mid 1840's Bingham turned almost exclusively to
genre, partly enabled to abandon portraiture through the purchase of his genre pictures by
the American Art Union. In 1844-1845 he sold four paintings to the Art Union, including his
masterly *Fur Traders Descending the Missouri* which brought seventy-five dollars. The
painting is almost exactly contemporaneous with Mount's *Eel Spearing at Setauket.* Each

depicts a characteristic scene of local life, has a hunting theme, and includes an older figure, a boy and a pet. In both pictures the boat, moving laterally over the calm water, is held steady by an oar. *The Fur Traders* is set early in the morning, as the mist slowly lifts from the river. Although it lacks the classical device of a pyramidal composition, the figures and the background are cleverly knit together. The head of the young half-breed is placed against a break in the trees, while the French trapper's cap marks the point where the lower level of trees on the distant shore meets the higher trees on what appears to be an island. The silhouette of the bear cub in the bow is bracketed diagonally between the motionless shapes of snags breaking the surface of the water in the foreground and middle distance. As in *Eel Spearing*, reflections in the water play an important role in completing the composition. The picture seems to capture the spirit of the river perfectly. During his career Bingham, the first major American artist to develop beyond the Alleghenies, created memorable images of the West that catch the essence of the locale and the character of the people, paralleling the achievement of Mount in the East.

Bingham's depictions of raftsmen, flatboatmen, and western politicians became widely known, especially through the engravings of his works distributed by the American Art Union. In a sense Mount and Bingham were history painters recording their own time. However they did not depict all aspects of their society. They chose leisure subjects, life's happy moments, and never dealt with the harsh severities of work or the less pleasant aspects of American existence. Bingham's raftsmen, for example, always appear at ease, dancing or fishing or playing cards, never at their arduous labor or pitting themselves against the elements.

Although Bingham's constant subject is life, a kaleidoscopic pattern of people and events, he usually presents it in quiescent, monumental images, with individual figures based on carefully worked drawings. The early *Fur Traders*, in which the direction of the action is parallel to the picture plane, appears motionless. However in his later river views, street scenes, and even the target range in *Shooting for the Beef* (1850, Brooklyn Museum, Brooklyn, New York) there are powerful diagonal recessions into space, conveying a sense of flux, of process. Bingham creates tension between the stasis of individual figures and the sweep of the composition that implies much about Americans, their rootedness and movement, in the nineteenth century.

To the student of American art Eastman Johnson (1824-1906) seems in retrospect to break like a false dawn in mid-nineteenth century painting, holding forth the promise of combining that grasp of the essence of American life found in the popular genre paintings of Mount and Bingham with a high degree of technical training and skill. Born in Maine and apprenticed at an early age to a Boston lithographer, Johnson made his initial reputation with highly realistic, almost photographic, pencil and crayon portraits of political and literary notables. In 1849 he went to Europe, studying, as did a number of American artists at mid-century (Bierstadt, Leutze, Whittredge) with Lessing in the Academy at Düsseldorf. He also worked at The Hague and Paris before returning to America in 1855. On the eve of the outbreak of the Civil War, Johnson painted in Washington, D.C. a scene of "negro life in the South," which now parades under the popular title *Old Kentucky Home*. The painting, marked by the tight handling and muted color that reflect his Düsseldorf training, was well received, and Johnson was elected an Academician of the National Academy of Design the following year. Whereas earlier paintings by artists as diverse as Copley and Mount had occasionally included a Negro as a picturesque figure, here the "different" figure is a white woman. She comes through an opening in the garden wall, leaving her elegant quarters to enter this picturesque place occupied by handsome, happy black people. One suspects that it contrasts favorably with her more genteel existence. The painting is reminiscent of Mount in its idealization of the Negro and the identification of the Negro with music. When Johnson settled in New York City in 1858, Mount was the old master of American genre painting, and still active in the academy. It seems extraordinary but nonetheless clear that

Mount, who never strayed far from rural Long Island, exerted a strong influence on the sophisticated Johnson. For example Johnson's *Corn Husking* of 1860 (Everson Museum of Art, Syracuse, New York) is obviously influenced by Mount's barn interior scenes, especially the *Banjo Player* of 1858 (Detroit Institute of Arts, Detroit, Michigan).

During the next few years Johnson produced a number of Civil War pictures, and after the war painted a colorful series of views of maple sugaring in his native Maine followed by some impressive mood-infused landscapes of Nantucket. During the latter part of his life Johnson abandoned genre painting entirely for a popular brand of comfortable portraiture. His early war and rural scenes are reminiscent of the work of his contemporary, Winslow Homer, and the later portraits resemble those of Thomas Eakins. But the resemblance is superficial, and Johnson's work never consistently rivaled the quality attained by Homer and Eakins, who between them carried the promise of an American art held forth by Mount and Bingham to fruition in the second half of the century. Standing midway in the history of American art between the towering figures of John Singleton Copley in the eighteenth century and Jackson Pollock in the twentieth century, Homer and Eakins are the twin peaks of American nineteenth century painting.

Eastman Johnson (1824-1906). Old Kentucky Home, 1859. (36×45″)
The New-York Historical Society, New York.

Winslow Homer (1836-1910) was raised in Cambridge, Massachusetts, then a delightful country village across the Charles River from Boston. At the age of nineteen he was apprenticed to John Bufford, a successful Boston lithographer. Young Homer soon began drawing pictures for publication (usually as wood engravings), sending the better ones to *Harper's Weekly* in New York. In 1859 he moved to New York as a freelance illustrator.

Homer covered Abraham Lincoln's inauguration for *Harper's* in 1861. When the Civil War broke out, he spent quite a bit of time as a correspondent at the front sketching. However few of his illustrations actually show military action. Homer preferred to concentrate on camp life, and his scenes are generally humorous or sentimental rather than stirring. As the war dragged on Homer became less concerned with it and more interested in his own artistic development. He was elected a member of the National Academy of Design in 1865 at the unusually early age of twenty-nine, and the following year exhibited his first popular success, *Prisoners from the Front* (Metropolitan Museum of Art, New York), a sympathetic representation of Southern prisoners standing before a young Union officer.

After the war Homer took up the pattern of artistic life familiar since the days of Thomas Cole and the Hudson River painters. When the weather turned fair, he traveled through New England, along the Hudson River, or down into Pennsylvania—hunting, fishing, camping and sketching. Back in New York he would develop his summer sketches into finished works during the winter. Although he lived in the city, the city itself was never his theme. His subjects were invariably rural, usually pleasant scenes involving women and children. Homer's early palette was subdued. The color areas on the picture surface are opaque, with dark background areas setting off a few brilliant touches of color in the foreground. Compositions revolve around a limited number of elements, the design simplified to large masses laid out in a flat decorative pattern, unmarred by niggling detail.

Although Homer, like Eastman Johnson, developed out of the genre tradition of Mount, he was more original in his response to it. Moving in a direction akin to Courbet and Naturalism, Homer divested his paintings of anecdote, choosing pictorial material for its own sake, free from the requirements of message or meaning.

Homer went to France for a year in 1866-1867, but the experience seems to have exerted remarkably little influence on him. Such influence as there was is more evident in the magazine illustrations on which he concentrated during the next six years than his paintings. His style became gayer and more fashionable, and marked by increased compositional daring that reflected increased awareness of Japanese prints. In 1873 Homer began to work in watercolor. Rarely have artist and medium been so well-suited. Watercolor permitted Homer to record direct observations of nature with freshness and immediacy, and he possessed the technical gifts to make the capricious medium increasingly responsive to his hand and his will. Watercolor demands sureness; when color touches paper, it is fixed. Homer reveled in the irreversible commitment of watercolor painting. Indeed watercolors became the cutting edge of his artistic growth. At first he simply used watercolors in place of pen and ink drawings as an improved method of preparing illustrations for publication, but increasingly he used them as initial sketches for oil paintings. Homer fought his artistic battles in watercolor skirmishes, carrying the resultant hard-won knowledge and skill over into his oils.

Homer's early paintings are generally sunlit scenes, often of young women playing croquet, or promenading along the seashore, or riding on horseback in the mountains. The women are invariably attractive, healthy, and fashionable, although aloof and impersonal. Figures are isolated from each other and from the viewer, and this isolation is sometimes intensified by anonymous male figures introduced in minor roles, their faces averted or hidden in shadow.

Although the adults in Homer's world seem isolated, his children frolic together in a cheerful world of laughter and mutuality. For Homer, growing up seems to imply a loss, a fall from paradise, removal from happy, carefree innocence and high spirits to a serious, lonely existence in which each man is an island unto himself. Homer's *Snap the Whip* (1872, Butler

Winslow Homer (1836-1910). Breezing Up, 1876. (24×38″)
National Gallery of Art, Washington, D.C. Gift of the W. L. and May T. Mellon Foundation.

Art Institute, Youngstown, Ohio) stands as a memorable image of childhood in rural America. If Bingham's scenes of life on the Mississippi caught the external appearance of the world of Huckleberry Finn, Homer's exuberant children at play convey the character of the boyhood days of Huck and Tom Sawyer. *Snap the Whip* is set in a sun-drenched valley, its bold diagonal recession echoed by the slanting line of the mountains and the roof of the schoolhouse. With thoughts of school far from their minds, the children hold hands to form a moving line anchored firmly at one end that snaps off at the other to send youngsters tumbling amidst the wildflowers.

Breezing Up is a seagoing version of *Snap the Whip*. The boys exert a mutual effort for their common delight. One adult is present, briefly privileged to share their pleasure. The day is sunny; the air and the water are alive. Wind fills the sails, and the boat fairly shudders as it drives through the choppy sea. The thrust of air against the canvas pulls every line taut, and all hands work to hold this living machine, quick with the breath of nature, under control. Lines are grasped firmly, the rudder is locked in place, and the figures throw their weight against the heave of the gunwhales to hold the boat under control as it skims along its course. In the right background a ship in full sail moves along the line of the horizon in serene counterpoint to the diagonal thrust of the foreground boat.

A salient characteristic of Homer's greatness as an artist is the capacity for change and growth manifested throughout his career, both in increased mastery over his artistic means and, more importantly, the artistic ends he made them serve. In the late 1870's one of Homer's periodic artistic transformations began. Homer spent greater amounts of time in close rapport with nature on fishing and hunting trips in the Adirondack Mountains and in

Winslow Homer (1836-1910). The Fog Warning, 1885. (30×48″)
Courtesy, Museum of Fine Arts, Boston, Massachusetts. Otis Norcross Fund.

Canada. The pattern of his existence seems in some ways a prolonged vacation, an attempt to perpetuate boyhood pleasures. Paintings of forest and mountain scenes became frequent. Homer devoted himself increasingly to watercolor, to a direct recording of nature, achieving ever more subtle atmospheric effects, the softening play of reflected lights, the coloristic linking of all parts into a pictorial unity replacing the clear separation of parts that characterized his earlier work.

In 1881 Homer, who had become increasingly anti-social, left America to spend two years in the English fishing village of Tynemouth on the North Sea. Life in Tynemouth was completely oriented toward the sea. The men fished; the women repaired the nets, raised the children, kept the house, and waited stoically on the strand for their men to return. Homer chose to concentrate on monumental figure studies of these sturdy and courageous women on the shore, rather than the perilous existence of the men at sea. He worked mostly in watercolor, seeking to master the dull diffuse atmosphere of the English coast. The sober tonality of these watercolors and the few oils of the period invoke an ominous feeling of the threat of the sea, which lurks behind every picture. From this time forward the sea becomes the dominant theme in Homer's work. On his return to America in 1883, he moved to Prout's Neck, a desolate fishing village on the coast of Maine, where he built a studio with a large balcony breasting the sea like a ship's bridge. This studio provided the solitude for which he felt an increasing need, and served as a base from which to launch his frequent excursions.

On his return to America Homer became intrigued with the subject of rescue from the sea, as his attention seemed to move slowly from the shore out to the sea itself. In *Lifeline* (1884, Philadelphia Museum of Art, Philadelphia, Pennsylvania), an unconscious female is transported to shore on a breeches buoy stretched between a foundering boat and a rocky coast, cradled in the arms of a man rendered anonymous by a red scarf that blows across his face. In *Undertow* (1886, Sterling and Francine Clark Art Institute, Williamstown, Massachusetts), two half-drowned young girls are dragged from the sea by lifeguards. The discipline Homer had developed in the Tynemouth watercolors strengthens the powerful and monumental oils of this period in which restrained, even dreary, color heightens the dramatic impact.

In 1884 Homer probably sailed with a fishing fleet, perhaps to the Grand Banks, and during the next two years he painted fishermen at sea in such monumental oils as *The Herring Nets* (1885, Art Institute of Chicago, Chicago, Illinois), *Eight Bells* (1886, Addison Gallery of American Art, Phillips Academy, Andover, Massachusetts) and *Fog Warning*. In *Fog Warning* a fisherman is alone at the end of the day on the open sea in a dory, his catch at his feet. He looks back over his left shoulder across the rolling waves at his ship, and gauges the intervening distance. Night is falling, and the fog is beginning to roll in. Will he have time to reach the safety of the ship before darkness and danger overtake him? His hands firmly grasp the oars, and his knowing glance makes it clear that he is in control of the situation. He pits his physical strength, his knowledge, his experience and his courage against the sea with the calm heroism that is a component part of his daily existence. The picture compositionally echoes *Breezing Up*. The boat moves diagonally into space to the left while a sailing ship moves to the right along the background horizon line. As in *Breezing Up* the boat is firmly under control, but there is a new seriousness of purpose. This is work, not play. This is a matter of life and death. The heroic theme demands and receives a monumentality of form that echoes the magnitude of the concept.

Winslow Homer (1836-1910). The Gulf Stream, 1899. (28⅛×49⅛″)

The Metropolitan Museum of Art, New York. Wolfe Fund, 1906.

89

As the years went by Homer continued to explore the theme of the relationship between man and nature. Each major painting required considerable thought and gestation, and his production of oils was limited to a few pictures each year. Almost all of Homer's previous *œuvre* seems pointed toward the climactic *Gulf Stream* of 1899. In this great painting Homer takes an unrelievedly grim view of existence in a deterministic universe. A Negro is adrift on the open sea. The mast of his sailing vessel has snapped. The rudder is gone. The composition echoes *Breezing Up* and *Fog Warning* but the theme has altered substantially. Here the human occupant exercises no control over the boat. It lies slack in the water, subject only to the will of the waves. In the right distance a menacing waterspout replaces the comforting sailing ships of the earlier pictures. There is a sailing vessel on the horizon, but to the left, moving beyond the listless Negro's line of vision. The ship and the solitary figure remain unaware of each other. Sharks circle the boat. A few touches of red color in the water at the stern, and dirty brown flotsam around the boat, add to the ominous mood of the scene. This man, this anonymous spark of life, is a pawn of forces beyond his control. He is at the mercy of an impersonal nature that does not care about him one way or the other. It may snuff him out, or it may not. The painting, produced one year after Stephen Crane's short story *The Open Boat*, is an exact pictorial counterpart to Crane's Naturalism. It echoes the view of the world expressed by Crane in a short poem in the same year, 1899.

> A man said to the universe:
> "Sir, I exist!"
> "However," replied the universe,
> "The fact has not created in me
> "A sense of obligation."

Although the final outcome of the scene in the painting is uncertain, the odds seem hopelessly stacked against the Negro. A contemporaneous watercolor by Homer (*After the Tornado*, 1899, Art Institute of Chicago, Chicago, Illinois) shows the body of a shipwrecked Negro thrown up on a sandy beach while the storm passes out to sea.

Gulf Stream marked the finale of an extended sequence of thematic paintings in which, consciously or unconsciously, Homer expressed his world view. The earlier paintings spoke of joyful commonality in the world of children, and hinted at adult loneliness made all the more poignant and bittersweet by the contrast. His paintings of the 1880's and 90's depicted men involved in cooperative efforts to earn a living or even simply to survive in the face of the dangers of the natural world. In these paintings Homer seems to imply that man's struggle with nature is what in fact establishes his humanity. It is what gives his life meaning. In a deterministic universe that is unconcerned about man or his fate, cooperation, the brotherhood of common effort, is what makes man human. Homer is not concerned with specific individuals. His people are anonymous, often to the point of having their faces hidden from view. The Negro in *Gulf Stream* is Everyman. He has no name, like Crane's characters—the cook, the oiler, the correspondent, the captain—in *The Open Boat*. A man joins the community of men not through peculiarly personal experiences, but through individually encountered common experiences.

Gulf Stream apparently drained Homer of what he had to say, and subsequently he concentrated on making pictures rather than statements. As Homer grew older his capacity for sustained growth did not end. Although he remained much of the time in relative isolation at Prout's Neck, remote from the centers of artistic life, his art during the first decade of the twentieth century was surprisingly advanced. He revealed an increasing interest in the formal possibilities of paintings, particularly color relationships, and the development of expressive forms which seem to parallel developments in German Expressionism during the same period. He was fascinated with unusual atmospheric effects, such as accompany a sunrise after a storm, and produced haunting visions of strangely colored seascapes with spume rising in wraithlike forms to dance along the rocky shore. His compositions became eccentric, reflecting a continuous, indeed increasing, responsiveness to Japanese prints. This is evident in his eerie *Kissing the Moon* (1904, Addison Gallery of

Winslow Homer (1836-1910). Right and Left, 1909. (28⅛×48½″)
National Gallery of Art, Washington, D.C. Gift of the Avalon Foundation.

American Art, Phillips Academy, Andover, Massachusetts) in which figures sit stiffly and without expression in a canoe dropping into the trough of an enormous wave which reaches up and almost seems to touch a low-hanging moon, echoing Hokusai's *Wave*.

Right and Left is one of Homer's oddest compositions. The point of view places the viewer floating free over the ocean, flying as it were in the company of ducks. In the distance a tiny figure in a boat, shrouded in mist, rises up and fires a double-barrelled shotgun blast in our direction. Before our eyes two ducks, one hit by each barrel, are splattered against the plane of their death, frozen momentarily in an ungainly sprawl. They resemble a naturalist's study, but Audubon would have shown the ducks in life, not death. Homer's subject is once more life and death, but here it seems to serve only as the point of departure for picturemaking. The startling result bears witness to the fact that Homer, despite his age, entered the twentieth century as a twentieth century artist.

Winslow Homer was an objective Realist, painting with detachment aspects of the real world that interested him and themes that embodied his thoughts on the meaning of life. His paintings rarely include his friends and never himself. Thomas Eakins (1844-1916) was, by contrast, a subjective Realist, passionately involved with the world in which he lived and which he painted. His art is a record of his life. Eakins was born in Philadelphia. His grandfather had been a weaver; his father was a drawing master. From them he inherited a tradition of craftsmanship, of precision, and, specifically from his father, a sense of drawing and its importance. Eakins shared his father's love of outdoor activities—sailing on the Delaware, rowing on the Schuylkill, swimming, hunting rail birds in the New Jersey marshes. Although he had a strong scientific inclination, he was primarily interested in art, and enrolled at the Pennsylvania Academy of Fine Arts. The Academy, with its collection of old history paintings by West and others, and plaster casts of antique statuary, was an unexciting place in which to study. However it did provide an opportunity to draw from living models. Surviving charcoal drawings by Eakins show nude female models masked to shield their identity, graphic witness to the local prudery that later blighted his career. Interested in learning all that he could about the human figure, Eakins concurrently studied anatomy at Jefferson Medical College, witnessing and participating in dissections.

In 1866, after the Civil War had ended, Eakins went to Paris to study. He enrolled in the Ecole des Beaux Arts, and chose to work in the studio of Jean-Léon Gérôme. Eakins' methodical artistic preparation—penmanship and mechanical drawing from his father, free drawing at the Pennsylvania Academy, anatomy at Jefferson Medical College—stood him in good stead at the conservative Ecole, still dominated by the shade of Ingres and his insistence on the primacy of draftsmanship. Eakins studied with Gérôme for over three years, and then in 1869 left Paris for Spain to paint on his own. There among the old masters he was deeply impressed by Ribera and Velasquez who, along with Rembrandt, he admired as forceful artists who painted "big work" with breadth and freedom.

Upon his return to Philadelphia in the summer of 1870, Eakins painted a number of intimate family portraits; dark, glowing images free of flattery and with emphasis on character and presence rather than specific detail. He resumed a vigorous outdoor life, and expanded his artistic subject matter to include this aspect of his days. In *Max Schmitt in a Single Scull* (1871, Metropolitan Museum of Art, New York), Eakins himself appears in a scull in the middle distance. These outdoor scenes, while informal in appearance, are in fact carefully structured distillations of the world in which the artist lived and breathed. Eakins often used preparatory drawings to establish a perspective grid on which every solid form could be locked in place. He brilliantly invoked the geometry of his compositions to heighten their pictorial impact. In his oil sketch of *John Biglin in a Single Scull* (1874, Yale University Art Gallery, New Haven, Connecticut) the horizon passes directly behind the rower's head. A vertical line drawn at right angles to the horizon at the vanishing point would pass just at the back of Biglin's profiled head, and directly through the oarlock. The oarlock is the fulcrum of the entire composition, the point at which all lines of arms, oars and struts converge, as well as the literal fulcrum for the rowing action depicted. Biglin, about to unleash his stroke, seems to brace his head against this invisible line, the curve of his back behind the line bent like an uncoiled spring, the arms and oars to the left of the line a rigid zigzag from shoulders to oarlock ready to execute the mechanics of the pull.

The 1876 painting of *Will Schuster and Blackman Going Shooting for Rail* is divided into three horizontal bands of sky, marsh and river, and three vertical strips, separated by the two standing figures, to form a gridlike "tic-tac-toe" composition. Upon this a triangle is superimposed, with the boat as the base and the Blackman's pole as one of the sides. The other side is an invisible line stretched tautly between the upper tip of the pole and the bow of the boat, passing through the lock of Will Schuster's cocked gun (reminiscent of the unseen vertical coordinate that passes through the oarlock in *John Biglin in a Single Scull*). The composition is knit tightly by a series of contrasts that begin with the juxtaposition of black man and white man. The value contrast of black trousers on the white man and white shirt on the black man is criss-crossed coloristically by the contrast of Will Schuster's red shirt and the black man's blue trousers. The vertical pole held by the black man balances the horizontal line of Schuster's gun.

A perspective grid supports this composition, permitting the major pictorial elements to be located with precision. Although the line of Will Schuster's gun and the gaze of the two figures run parallel to and assert the picture plane, the boat diverges into pictorial space, stretching open the composition. The heft of the Negro presses the back of the boat into the water and raises the bow. As he leans his weight against the pole to hold the boat motionless, the boat tips toward the picture plane. The accurate response of the boat to the physical forces acting upon it emphasizes dramatically that the base of the dominant compositional triangle, the boat, is a skitterish thing held steady on the water for a

Thomas Eakins (1844-1916). Will Schuster and Blackman Going Shooting for Rail, 1876. (22⅛×30¼″)
Yale University Art Gallery, New Haven, Connecticut. Bequest of Stephen Carlton Clark, B.A. 1903.

breathless moment while Schuster takes aim. Anticipation is screwed to an excruciating pitch by the viewer's awareness that the whole taut equilibrium is precarious. The least twitch or jostle will throw the gun out of line, and the shot will miss. The hammer is back, attention is focused on the unseen target to the left, everything awaits the release that will come when the trigger is pulled. The release is implied visually by the puff of green foliage near the mouth of the gun and the brown tree limb tracing the trajectory of the shot. Eakins caught, or one might say constructed, the synthetic moment that sums up all that has gone before—the movement of the boat through the marshes, the flushing of the bird, the balancing of the boat, the sighting of the gun—and implies what is to follow. This is the moment of potency. Thus Eakins perceives, imparts order to, and records his world. It is very different from the more purely pictorial concern of Homer's *Right and Left*, where the results of a shot are orchestrated into a remarkable image free from thematic overtones.

Eakins had resumed his study of anatomy at Jefferson Medical College upon his return to Philadelphia. Just as mechanical drawing permitted him to construct an armature for his realistic views of the world around him, so knowledge of anatomy led to more realistic delineations of human beings. His study led directly to the painting of *The Gross Clinic*, one of the major monuments in the history of American art. The painting represents Dr. Samuel Gross, the dominant figure at Jefferson Medical College, in his dual role as surgeon and teacher. Standing as Eakins had often seen him in the somber amphitheater, light flooding

93

down from a skylight above, Gross is operating on the leg of a patient. He has made an incision, and while his associates hold the cut open, he turns to his students to explain what has been done and what he is about to do. His bloodied hand grasps the scalpel, the cruel cold fact of its work more than balanced by the compassion and objective professionalism of the man.

The Gross Clinic immediately recalls *The Anatomy Lesson of Dr. Tulp* by Rembrandt, one of Eakins' artistic heroes. Both paintings are portrait groups on the theme of medical instruction, although *The Gross Clinic* represents an operation on a live patient rather than the dissection of a cadaver. *The Gross Clinic* also contains echoes of several of the more popular paintings of gladiatorial combat and Christian martyrdom by Eakins' erstwhile teacher, Gérôme, in which spectators similarly witness a bloody scene of laceration, pain and possible death in a circular arena. However, Eakins' picture is neither anecdotal nor sentimental. It is a frank record of a drama of contemporary life. It is not pleasant to watch, and the viewer sympathizes with the mother of the patient seated on the left who shields her eyes with her arms, her hands clutching at the air in anguish. But the picture is humane too. The figure of Gross, kindly and knowing, dominates the scene, making it clear that dispassionate science and technical skill are servant to humane wisdom and compassion.

The blunt honesty of *The Gross Clinic* shocked and offended Eakins' contemporaries. The painting was rejected for the art section of the Philadelphia Centennial Exhibition of 1876, for which it had been painted, and Eakins was forced to exhibit it in the medical pavilion. The public, comfortable with anecdotal paintings, able to gaze with equanimity at the bloodiest *Massacres of the Innocents* or the most revolting scenes of flayed, crucified, beheaded or roasted martyrs as long as the event took place long ago and far away, was shocked and offended by a representation of bloodshed, suffering, pain and grief in contemporary Philadelphia. Outraged critics objected to what they felt was gratuitous brutality. This kind of picture was not elevating to the morals, instructive to the mind, enlightening to the spirit, or even divertingly anecdotal. What could be the justification of brutal realism for its own sake? Few understood that Eakins had taken American painting an important step further along its traditional path of realism, opening up increased possibilities for the honest and free recording of the realities of contemporary life.

In *The Gross Clinic* Eakins sought the synthetic moment, just as in *Will Schuster and Blackman Going Shooting for Rail*. Gross, turning from his operation to talk to his students, is characterized both as gifted surgeon and magnetic teacher. The dual emphasis on the bloody hand and the intelligent, compassionate face, weathered by experience, captures the essence of the man.

The negative public response to *The Gross Clinic* marked only the beginning of Eakins' troubles. As teacher of the life classes at the Pennsylvania Academy of Fine Arts from 1877, Eakins stressed the importance of drawing from undraped models. He believed that a thorough understanding of anatomy was prerequisite to the accurate picturing of pose and locomotion. Unfortunately his enthusiastic and graphic instruction in the facts of comparative anatomy, using live models, shocked some of the more conventional female pupils. A devoted and inspired teacher, loved by his professional students, Eakins suffered a great blow when he was dismissed from his post at the Academy because of his insistent use of nude models before mixed classes.

As a realist who was interested in anatomically correct depictions of the nude human figure, Eakins was hard put to find subject matter in contemporary life which included undraped figures. His choice of scenes of rowing, boxing and surgical operations partially reflects his interest in anatomy. Even his depiction of a *Crucifixion* (1880, Philadelphia Museum of Art, Philadelphia, Pennsylvania) resulted from his interest in an anatomical study of the human body under stress rather than any religious sentiments. Opportunities to depict nude or partially nude females were particularly limited in Victorian Philadelphia. However, perhaps motivated by the general climate of retrospective historical awareness that accompanied the centennial celebration, Eakins did discover a pretext for painting a

Thomas Eakins (1844-1916). The Gross Clinic, 1875. (96×78″)
Courtesy of the Jefferson Medical College, Philadelphia, Pennsylvania.

nude female in a subject taken from the artistic history of Philadelphia itself, *William Rush Carving His Allegorical Figure of the Schuylkill River* (1877, Philadelphia Museum of Art, Philadelphia, Pennsylvania). When Rush, a Philadelphia sculptor of the late eighteenth and early nineteenth centuries, had required a model to pose nude for an allegorical statue commissioned by the City of Philadelphia, and encountered the same prudery that later frustrated Eakins, he resolved the problem by getting the daughter of a local merchant to pose with a chaperone in constant attendance. Eakins ingeniously resolved his problem by painting an historical reminiscence of Rush at work, a subject that was local and factual, if not contemporary, and afforded him an opportunity to paint a female nude. Eakins subsequently returned to this pictorial device several times, treating the same subject in a variety of compositions.

Eakins' interest in anatomy led to an increasing concern with motion. In the *Swimming Hole* of 1882 (Fort Worth Art Center, Fort Worth, Texas), Eakins depicts a group of friends diving and swimming in the nude, while he himself treads water in the lower right hand corner and looks on, the constant observer. Eakins was also interested in animal loco-motion. For the picture of *Fairman Rogers' Four-in-Hand* (1879, Philadelphia Museum of Art, Philadelphia, Pennsylvania), he made extensive studies, including wax models, of horses in motion (one of a number of interesting parallels between Eakins and Degas). An expert photographer, he became interested in Eadweard Muybridge's experiments in motion photography, and experimented himself with multiple exposure photographs of athletes in motion.

During his later years, although generally recognized as an important American artist, Eakins received few honors and few commissions. His battles over realism of subject matter and nudity in art made him, in Lloyd Goodrich's phrase, something of "an artistic outlaw." Although his art was neglected by the public, Eakins' artistic thinking, abetted by his warm personality, became the dominant influence on the next generation of American realists, notably the artists of the so-called "Ashcan School." His friend Walt Whitman recognized his potency when he said, "Tom Eakins is not a painter, he is a force." The basic thrust of Eakins' art and his teaching was in the direction of heightened realism. He strove for accuracy in reproducing external reality through his mastery of perspective drawing, human anatomy, and locomotion, and in capturing internal reality as well, probing for essences, whether in the representation of the synthetic moment of a scene or in rendering probing character studies that reveal the record of a life lived in lines and wrinkles, glance and pose.

Although both Homer and Eakins spent a few years in Europe, almost all of their major work was done in America. A third American painter, Albert Pinkham Ryder (1847-1917), although representing the opposite end of the artistic spectrum as a non-realist, must be classified with Homer and Eakins as a major native artist who hammered out solutions to his artistic problems in America rather than in Europe. Like them too, Ryder dealt with significant artistic problems, although his output was limited and his paintings generally small. Ryder was born in New Bedford, Massachusetts, on Cape Cod, then the largest whaling port in the world. As a self-taught artist, Ryder was frustrated in his early attempts to record the myriad details of the natural world. An infinitude of leaves and branches perplexed him. Suddenly, one day, he saw natural objects in terms of their essential form, and, working more with palette knife than brush, he re-created these forms on canvas in a way that was more satisfying and in essence more accurate than his more detailed previous attempts.

In 1870 Ryder moved to New York where he continued to paint landscapes, often not from nature but from recollection of the scenes he had known in Massachusetts. These landscapes were usually bathed with the soft golden sunlight of late afternoon or silvery moonlight, rather than the full light of midday, yielding a serene, dream-like quality to the results. Although he exhibited occasionally at the National Academy, and was a founding member of the Society of American Artists in 1877, Ryder was largely ignored by public and

Museum of Art, New York). The madman seemed to dwell in a different world, removed from our own. Ryder, an apparent Platonist, was similarly interested in the ideal world that lay behind the illusory screen of the physical real world. His remarkably fragile and lovely *The Dead Bird* of 1890-1900, atypical in theme and handling, depicts a lifeless yellow bird against a thinly painted yet textured background. The wood panel shows irregularly through the pigment, and gives the effect that the lifeless bird is literally lying crumpled on its surface. Around the bird a ridge of paint traces the outline of a larger, ghostly bird form, that seems to stand almost as a bird spirit behind the inert body. The painting is a still life of death, literally a *nature morte*, in which the composition is focused on a single object, an object with no life force of its own. The viewer is forced into an intimate confrontation with the lifeless form of the bird and the echoing bird shape behind, into inescapable speculation on the meaning of life and death.

To get at the underlying reality of the noumenal world that lurks behind phenomena, the world perhaps accessible through the conjectures of a madman, the memories of children, the vision of mystics, dreams, or the probing imagination of artists, Ryder strove to reduce forms to their essences. The natural world was important to Ryder not for its own

Albert Pinkham Ryder (1847-1917). The Race Track or Death on a Pale Horse, 1895-1910. (28¼×35¼")
Cleveland Museum of Art, Cleveland, Ohio. Purchase, J. H. Wade Fund.

Albert Pinkham Ryder (1847-1917). The Dead Bird, 1890-1900.
The Phillips Collection, Washington, D.C.

critics alike. After 1880 his paintings became increasingly imaginative. His paintings on
biblical themes, with their expressive distortions, revealed a genuine, if unorthodox,
religious sensibility. Often a literary or poetic theme provided the point of departure. The
great English poets were a major source of inspiration, notably Chaucer (*Constance*, before
1876, Boston Museum of Fine Arts, Boston, Massachusetts) and Shakespeare (*Macbeth and
the Witches*, 1890, Phillips Collection, Washington, D.C.; *The Forest of Arden*, 1877, Metropolitan Museum of Art, New York; *The Tempest*, before 1891, The Detroit Institute of Arts,
Detroit, Michigan). He admired contemporary Romantic poets like Byron, Moore, Campbell
and Tennyson, and also found inspiration in Romantic music. Several of his paintings were
inspired by the operas of Richard Wagner, including *The Flying Dutchman* (1887, National
Collection of Fine Arts, Smithsonian Institution, Washington, D.C.), and *Siegfried and the
Rhine Maidens* (1875-1891, National Gallery of Art, Washington, D.C.) which he began late
one night after hearing the opera, and worked on for forty-eight hours without sleep or food
until he had it largely done (although as with many of his paintings he later reworked it).

Perhaps the strongest influence on Ryder was exerted by Edgar Allan Poe, whose
fevered imagination was akin to his own. *The Temple of the Mind* of 1885 (Albright-Knox
Art Gallery, Buffalo, New York) was based on Poe's poem, *The Haunted Palace* from *The
Fall of the House of Usher*. The painting was acquired immediately after its completion by
the first major collector of American art, Thomas B. Clarke. This helped to establish
Ryder's reputation, and created a demand for his work that he could not satisfy because of
his slowness and his reluctance to relinquish his paintings. *The Temple of the Mind* depicts a
temple in a state of ruinous decay. Outside, three graces, former occupants of the temple,
wait for a "weeping love" to join them. A cloven-footed faun dances up the path to the
ruined temple, snapping his fingers in glee at having dethroned the erstwhile ruling graces.
Ryder's meaning here goes beyond a comment on the cycle of grandeur and decay such as is
found in Thomas Cole's *The Course of Empire*. Here the temple symbolizes a body deserted
by the mind, an empty shell, about to be occupied by demonic madness. In the second half
of the nineteenth century the theme of madness engaged the attention of a number of the
more imaginative painters (e.g. Elihu Vedder's *The Lost Mind*, 1864-1865, Metropolitan

sake, but as a point of departure, the available evidence which had to be probed and pondered and made transparent. Ryder spent long hours in silent communion with nature, often walking late at night around New York and nearby New Jersey, soaking up the effects of moonlight on clouds. Images from the natural world were ingested by Ryder, steeped in his subconscious for long periods of time, their details falling away to leave only the essential form, divested of anything accidental or meaningless. This is what reappeared in his paintings—a tree that conveys the essential form of treeness, a boat that is the quintessence of boatiness, clouds that are archetypal clouds encircling the mooniest of moons. Sometimes dark and fuzzy, the forms are solid and irreducible at the core. *Toilers of the Sea* (Metropolitan Museum of Art, New York), exhibited in 1884, is free of all irrelevant detail. Sailboat, sea, clouds and moon are archetypal images. The picture bears a strong compositional similarity to Homer's *Fog Warning* of the following year, which also treats the theme of a fisherman on the open sea returning home at the end of the day. However the two pictures are completely different conceptually. One is detailed and realistic, with the situation clearly stated; the other is obscure, mysterious and dreamlike.

Ryder's own creative symbolism came into play in an extraordinary painting, *The Race Track* of 1895-1910. It was evoked by the suicide of an acquaintance, a waiter in his brother's Brooklyn hotel, who had foolishly plunged all of his life's savings in a wager on a horse race, lost, and committed suicide. Ryder combines the theme of a horse running on a deserted country track with the more profound image of a mounted grim reaper who rides as one of the Horsemen of the Apocalypse. There are prototypes for this kind of apocalyptic vision in American art, notably Benjamin West's *Death on a Pale Horse* (final version, 1817, Pennsylvania Academy of Fine Arts, Philadelphia, Pennsylvania) and Rembrandt Peale's *Court of Death* (1820, The Detroit Institute of Arts, Detroit, Michigan), but these are large pictorial machines very different from Ryder's more personal conception. Although the barren setting of *The Race Track* seems hauntingly familiar, it is more like a dreamscape than a natural landscape. A skeletal tree behind the rider attests to the fruitlessness of this place. The serpent slithering along the ground is a reminder of the temptation that lures man into foolishness. Everything appears an inversion of normalcy, yielding an image of a dreamworld, actually a nightmare world, that lies behind the familiar world of phenomena. It appears to be night, the time of dreams, although the hour is uncertain and Ryder claimed that he never gave any thought as to whether it was day or night in the painting. The tree is leafless, the mounted figure fleshless, the track is deserted, the unearthly horse floats weightlessly above the turf, circling clockwise, against the grain of an American race course. All is inverted in this realm of unpleasant Ideas, this nightmare noumenal world.

Ryder's total production of paintings was limited. He let pictures develop over long periods of time. Painting often on small wooden panels, he laid layer upon layer, often working impatiently on wet surfaces to achieve a sensuous richness of effect. He at times introduced unstable media, such as wax, candlegrease and alcohol, and his uncraftsmanly practices have caused many of his paintings to deteriorate badly. In his late years Ryder became markedly eccentric, and much more of a recluse than Winslow Homer. His apartment in lower Manhattan was filled with debris, through which paths led to his easel, a window, a mat on the floor upon which he slept, a fireplace, with festoons of wallpaper hanging from the ceiling. Ryder's powers fell off in his later years, and he kept reworking a number of earlier paintings to their physical detriment. He was, however, befriended by and influential upon some younger artists, notably Marsden Hartley, who admired his highly personal creations.

Imaginative painting has been a constant companion to the stronger tradition of realism in American art. Indeed during the first half of the nineteenth century, under the pervasive influence of Romanticism, art of the imagination achieved qualitative, if not quantitative, pre-eminence in the works of Allston and Cole. Although Mount, Bingham, Homer and Eakins subsequently reasserted the dominance of Realism, imaginative painting continued to flourish in the second half of the century in the hands of Ryder, William Page (1811-1885), Elihu Vedder (1836-1923), Thomas W. Dewing (1851-1938), George Fuller (1822-1884), and John La Farge (1835-1910).

One of the most gifted of the imaginative artists in the nineteenth century was the landscape painter George Inness (1825-1894). Born in Newburgh, New York, Inness began to paint in 1842 in the late Hudson River School landscape tradition, instructed briefly by the little known Regis Gignoux (1816-1882), but influenced primarily by Durand and Cole. In 1847 he traveled to England and Italy, and in subsequent years returned to Europe regularly. His artistic development is clearly marked by influences of contemporary European painting, especially the landscapes of the Barbizon School. His early landscapes were quite detailed and naturalistic. Later his scenes became progressively more moody and atmospheric. His brushwork became softer, outlines more fluid, and forms less architectural. In this sense, the pattern of this work follows that of the great French landscapist J. B. C. Corot, whom he admired. After 1875 Inness gained increasing fame and prosperity, particularly through the patronage of the first great collector of American art, T. B. Clarke.

In his late years Inness' style became still more vaporous and unworldly, largely as a result of his increasingly intense religious mysticism and his involvement with Swedenborgianism. In the *Home of the Heron* (1891, Art Institute of Chicago) and *Indian Summer*, painted in the last year of his life, misty forms float rootlessly over a landscape vaguely reminiscent of the natural world, suggesting some sort of transcendent Swedenborgian vision.

George Inness (1825-1894). Indian Summer, 1894. (45¼×30″)

Mr. George M. Curtis Collection, Clinton, Iowa.

Another artist working in a more imaginative vein was Ralph Albert Blakelock (1847-1919), who has often been understandably but inaccurately linked with Ryder because of stylistic similarities. Although Ryder and Blakelock were exact contemporaries in New York City, they worked quite independently. Born into comfortable circumstances in New York, the son of a physician, Blakelock began to exhibit landscapes at the National Academy of Design in 1867. He was in the West between 1869 and 1872, and his subsequent artistic career was profoundly affected by this experience. Indian life and its landscape setting became his recurrent theme. Subsequently he almost invariably traced an arrowhead outline around the signature on his paintings. Unlike many painters of the American Indian, Blakelock's interest was not anthropological or factual. For Blakelock the Indian was the ancient and natural inhabitant of America; this place belongs authentically to the Indian, and his spirit and the spirit of the land are one. During much of the nineteenth century, after Enlightenment theories about the "Noble Savage" had faded in the face of real experience and national priorities, the Indian was considered a vile threat that had to be annihilated as America expanded westward to fulfil her "Manifest Destiny." But later in the century, rendered harmless, the Indian began once more to be appreciated. Blakelock was in the van of this revised view, along with Bierstadt who suggested the same sort of harmony between the Indian and the western landscape. The process of idealization was carried further in the work of Thomas Moran (1837-1926) and George De Forest Brush (1855-1941) at the end of the century. It became pervasive in the work of such diverse twentieth century artists as Robert Henri, John Marin, Georgia O'Keeffe, Frank Lloyd Wright and an entire school of painters at Taos, New Mexico, all of whom found meaningful American roots in the Indians and their land.

Blakelock, like Ryder, rarely depicted scenes in full daylight, and often painted moonlight scenes. Blakelock's range of themes was much more restricted than Ryder's. He dealt with landscape almost exclusively, drawing little or no inspiration from literature. However he was even more responsive to music. Ryder was inspired more by operatic themes than by the music, whereas Blakelock, a skilled pianist, often improvised on the piano, searching for color compositions and pictorial ideas. This kind of synesthesia, in which sounds suggested pictorial possibilities, was to become an important element in opening the way to pure abstraction in the late nineteenth and early twentieth centuries, from the "Nocturnes" and "Symphonies" of Whistler to the "Synchromies" of Morgan Russell and Stanton Macdonald-Wright.

Like Ryder, Blakelock also had a strongly developed sense of the physical properties of the material with which he worked. He was particularly conscious of the surfaces of his pictures, working them over and scraping them to achieve desired textural effects. Again like Ryder he used unstable materials, mixing varnish and bitumen with his pigments, which has caused his paintings to darken and crinkle over the years.

As is evident in his masterly *Moonlight*, Blakelock was concerned with the decorative treatment of the picture surface and did not share Ryder's preoccupation with the creation of solid irreducible forms. A decorative veil of trees frames an opening in the center of the picture through which the eye proceeds from the warm foreground to the cooler tonalities in the distance.

Blakelock married in 1877, and his family grew rapidly. With nine children eventually to support, he was under increasing pressure to secure income. Prices for his pictures were low, and he began to crank out repetitive images to earn a few dollars. Rebuffed by patrons and ignored by critics, Blakelock began to crack under the strain. It is said that in 1891, with a child about to be born, Blakelock went with a recently completed picture to a patron who had previously bought his work. The man offered Blakelock one half the asking price for the picture, and admonished Blakelock that if he did not accept the offer, it would be lower later on. Blakelock declined, was then unable to sell the picture elsewhere, and ultimately returned to the original patron and was forced to accept the lower price for the picture. Shortly afterward, Blakelock was found wandering in the streets tearing up one

Ralph Albert Blakelock (1847-1919). Moonlight, about 1885. (27¼×32¼″)
The Brooklyn Museum, Brooklyn, New York.

hundred dollar bills. He was temporarily placed in an asylum. After his release he became increasingly eccentric, affecting Indian dress of sashes, beads and richly embroidered belts, along with long hair and beard. When he was incarcerated permanently in 1899 he had delusions of great wealth. Indeed prices for his paintings did rise sharply thereafter, but no benefit accrued to him or to his family. In 1912 *Moonlight*, which Blakelock was originally going to sell for $50 but for which an artist friend had gotten $600, changed hands for $13,900, the highest price paid up to that time for the work of a living American artist. As prices rose, Blakelock's paintings, like those of Ryder, were extensively forged, and the problem of Blakelock attributions has been a serious one for subsequent scholars.

Several specialized categories of nineteenth century painting stand outside of the mainstream of American art, and yet are important constituent parts of the total artistic enterprise in America. A few of these special categories, for instance folk art and the work of artist-naturalists, have already been discussed. Another discrete realm of American nineteenth century painting, shaped, indeed created, by the taste for realism, is *trompe l'œil* painting. An interest in hyper-realism, in paintings so real that they deceive the viewer into confusing painted reality with actual reality, has already been noted in connection with Copley's American portraits and Charles Willson Peale's *Staircase Group*. *Trompe l'œil* painting flourished in America during the nineteenth century, especially in Philadelphia, in a tradition shaped and furthered by the Peale family. Charles Willson Peale's son, Raphaelle Peale (1774-1825), was a master of *trompe l'œil* painting, and indeed one of the best of all American still life painters.

Apparently Raphaelle Peale had a termagant wife who kept poking around his studio. In a delightful attempt to teach his wife a lesson, and to keep her out of his studio, Peale painted the amusing and extraordinarily effective *After the Bath* of 1823. One can almost imagine Peale's wife entering his studio in his absence to find unframed on the easel a canvas apparently representing a nude drying her hair after bathing. A linen cloth hanging from a tape over the surface of the picture concealed everything but a partial view of arm and hair above and a foot poking out below. Her suspicions confirmed, did she attempt to snatch the towel off, only to find that it was all a painted illusion, linen, tape and all? Yes or no, it is a wonderful story and an effective painting.

The greatest master of American *trompe l'œil* painting was William M. Harnett (1848-1892). However a number of other extremely gifted *trompe l'œil* painters also worked during the latter part of the nineteenth century, notably John F. Peto (1854-1907) and John Haberle (1856-1933). Harnett's *Faithful Colt* of 1890, like Peale's *After the Bath*, is a superlatively beautiful as well as effectively deceptive painting. With extraordinary skill the artist has caught the exact appearance of the hammered, rust-flecked barrel of the gun contrasting with the more finely grained brass of the trigger guard and the cracked ivory handle. The painted vertical planks in the background are splintered, and beneath rusty nails and nailholes washes of rust stain drift down. A clipping pasted to the wall in the lower right undulates ever so slightly, and the viewer can hardly resist the temptation to pull it off by a curling corner. Unable to sign his name in a normal fashion on the picture surface without destroying the integrity of the image, Harnett inscribed it in the lower left so that his name and the date appear to have been carved into the surface of the plank with a penknife. Harnett's realistic depiction of things is not unrelated to Eakins' probing representations of people, places and events, similarly produced in Philadelphia at about the same time.

In addition to the dazzling competence of the technique, Harnett also achieved a perfect balance of pictorial parts in the sharply limited space, so that the abstract quality of the design is extraordinarily effective. In tribute to Harnett's remarkable ability and popularity, his work was not only imitated but industrious attempts were made to pass off as original Harnetts the work of other artists. Obviously technical requirements ruled out crude imitations. Some years ago the scholar Alfred Frankenstein noted that signed Harnett paintings tended to fall into two quite disparate categories: those painted in a "hard" style such as the *Faithful Colt* in which the forms are crisp, textures are clearly differentiated, details are recreated with microscopic accuracy, the image has a strong tactile appeal, space is severely limited, objects occasionally project into the spectator's space, and a clear spatial relationship of the parts obtains; all in contrast to a "soft" style in which all of these characteristics except limited depth are reversed, and in which textures are homogeneous and soft, colors strong, and light-dark contrasts more marked. These paintings have a moodier and more sentimental quality, showing objects evocative of human use and associations, such as a pile of old books, called *Discarded Treasures* (Smith College Museum of Art, Northampton, Massachusetts), or a littered desk entitled *After Night's Study* (Detroit Institute of Arts, Detroit, Michigan). Frankenstein's investigations revealed that the "hard" style was Harnett's own, but that the "soft" pictures were works by Peto to which Harnett's signature had been added.

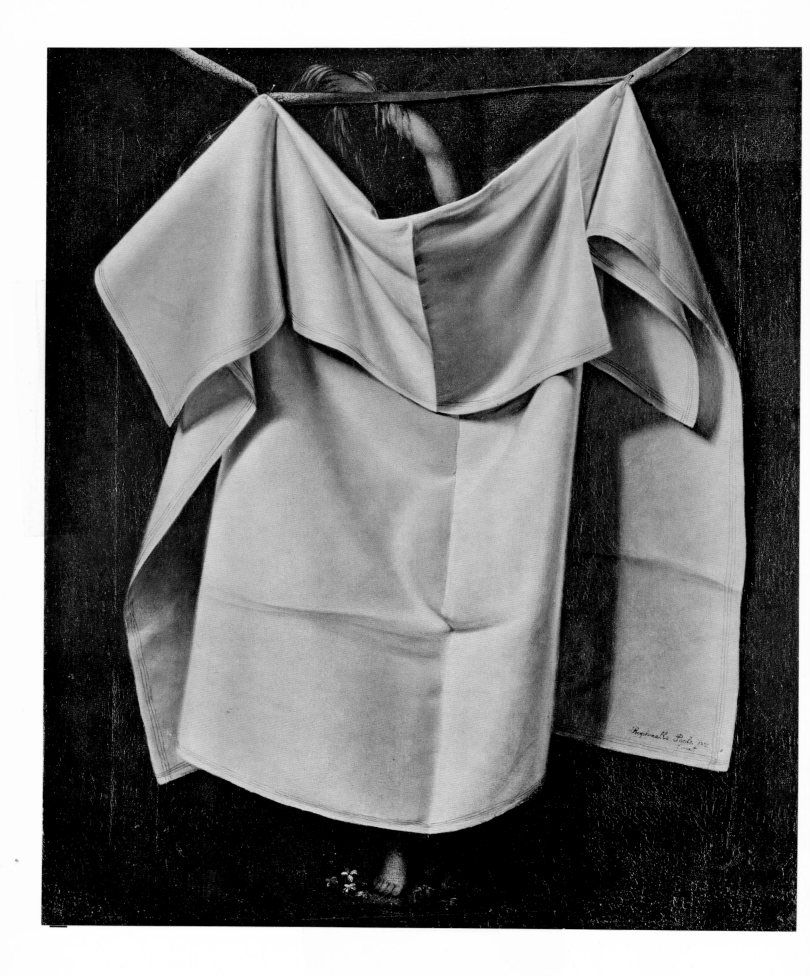

Raphaelle Peale (1774-1825). After the Bath, 1823. (29×24″)
Nelson Gallery-Atkins Museum (Nelson Fund), Kansas City, Missouri.

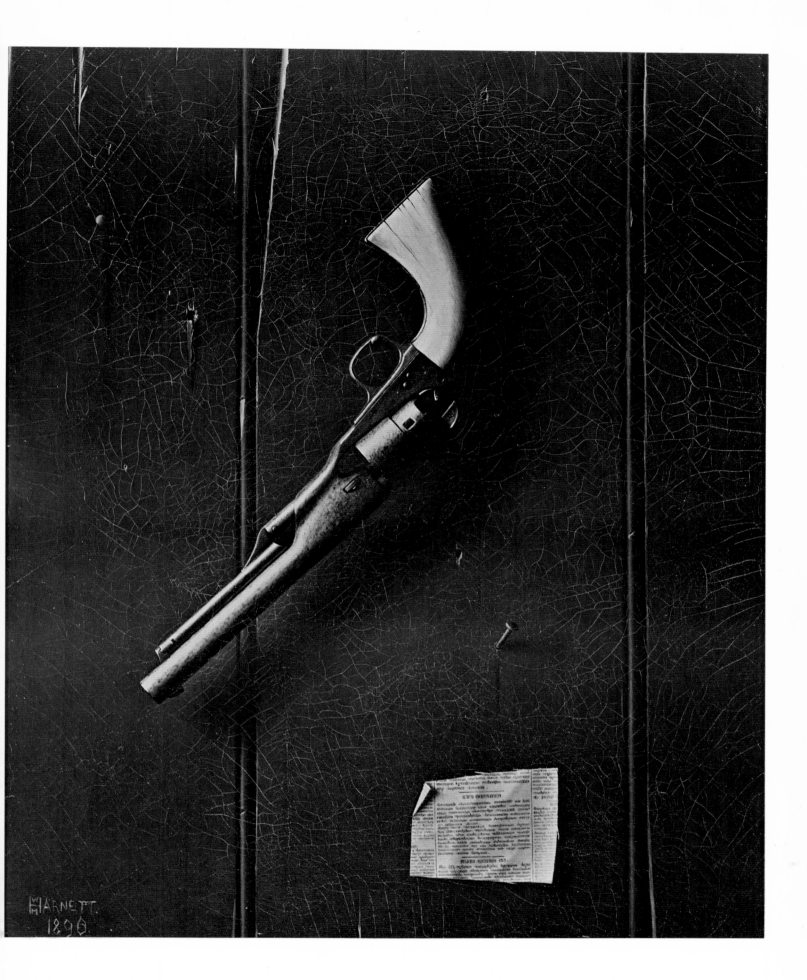

William M. Harnett (1848-1892). The Faithful Colt, 1890. (22½×19″)

Wadsworth Atheneum, Hartford, Connecticut. The Ella Gallup Sumner and Mary Catlin Sumner Collection.

Charles Marion Russell (1864-1926). Crippled But Still Coming, 1913. (30×48")
Amon Carter Museum of Western Art, Fort Worth, Texas.

Another special and definable classification, already briefly considered in the work of
Bierstadt and Blakelock, is the art of the West. In the nineteenth century, as westward
expansion of the United States compressed the Indians into limited land areas, it became
increasingly apparent that their way of life, indeed perhaps their very existence, was
doomed to extinction. After the Louisiana Purchase of 1803, and the Lewis and Clark
Expedition the following year, which opened up the still largely unexplored territories
between the Missouri River and the Pacific coast, ever-increasing numbers of Americans
moved westward. Expeditions not infrequently included artists among their complement,
and their pictorial records are often of extraordinary historic interest, even when low in
artistic quality.

The first artist of real stature to go West was George Catlin (1796-1872). Born in
Wilkes-Barre, Pennsylvania, he was educated as a lawyer and for several years practiced in
Philadelphia. A self-taught artist, he painted at first only as an amateur, but by the time he
was thirty he had established himself as a successful portrait painter and gave up the law.
Sensing that the Indian was doomed, Catlin took it as his purpose "to rescue from oblivion
the looks and customs of the vanishing races of the native man in America."

During the early 1830's Catlin traveled all over the West, often alone on horseback and
by canoe, penetrating into unmapped territories and visiting forty-eight tribes. Living with
them, acquiring their languages, familiarizing himself with their customs and way of life
(which, as he foresaw, were on the verge of extinction), he made many portraits of Indians,
such as the superb *The White Cloud, Head Chief of the Iowas*, and countless sketches of
Indian life. Subsequently he exhibited his collection of Indian paintings and paraphernalia

in the cities along the east coast of America, and in the 1840's took the exhibition to London and Paris, lecturing on Indians and championing their cause. Several of his Indian portraits were shown at the Paris Salon of 1846, where they were seen by Charles Baudelaire, the most discerning art critic of the day, who commented on them admiringly: "Catlin has rendered superlatively well the proud free character and noble expression of these splendid fellows; the structure of their heads has been thoroughly understood. With their fine attitudes and easy movements, these savages make antique sculpture comprehensible. As for the coloring, there is something mysterious about it that delights me more than I can say." The bulk of Catlin's great collection of Indian pictures is now preserved in the Smithsonian Institution and the National Gallery of Art in Washington.

The greatest of all western artists, and indeed the most valuable visual source for the history of the West, despite his late appearance on the scene, was Frederic Remington (1861-1909). Extraordinarily accurate in his depictions, and uniting a genuine artistic talent with deep understanding of his subject, Remington produced over 3000 pictures that, more than the work of any other artist, shape our memory of the Golden West. *A Dash for Timber* of 1899 is an extraordinary example of the vitality of his art, reflecting something of Eakins' concern with reality, but overlaid with a sense of excitement and energy that Eakins intentionally filtered out of his static and synthetic images. Indeed many of the western artists themselves were vigorous outdoor types who lived what they painted. The archetype of the artist-cowboy was Charles Marion ("Charlie") Russell (1864-1926) of Montana. Lured to the far west from his boyhood home in St. Louis by the romantic appeal of a life of high adventure and freedom from the restraints of civilization, the doughty and colorful Russell made his way first by punching cattle and then increasingly by painting pictures such as *Crippled But Still Coming* of 1913. Actually, with few exceptions, the art of the West falls

Frederic Remington (1861-1900). A Dash for Timber, 1899. (48¾×84⅜″)
Amon Carter Museum of Western Art, Fort Worth, Texas.

George Catlin (1796-1872). The White Cloud, Head Chief of the Iowas. (27¾×22¾″)
National Gallery of Art, Washington, D.C. Paul Mellon Collection.

into the broader category of American realist painting, and the overriding concern of most artists of the West with accuracy in the depiction of Indians and Indian life is a manifestation of the deeply rooted American predilection for realism. This new realism of immediacy and motion combined with the Philadelphia tradition of realism reaching from the Peales to Harnett and Eakins to inspire what came to be called the "Ashcan School," a group of artists who aggressively projected the tradition of realism in American art into the twentieth century, expanding the thematic limits of their art to encompass the immediate feel of contemporary American life. However other American artists working abroad were simultaneously pursuing very different ends, concerning themselves more with the formal properties of art itself than with its relevance to real life. The ultimate confrontation between these opposed concepts of art was to become the lead story in the history of American art during the twentieth century.

James Abbott McNeill Whistler (1834-1903). Nocturne in Black and Gold: The Falling Rocket, about 1874. (23¾×18⅜")
The Detroit Institute of Arts, Detroit, Michigan.

From Art for the Sake of Art
to the Ashcan School

I HAVE seen, and heard, much of Cockney impudence before now; but never expected to hear a coxcomb ask two hundred guineas for flinging a pot of paint in the public's face," wrote John Ruskin about James A. McNeill Whistler (1834-1903) and his *Nocturne in Black and Gold: The Falling Rocket* when the picture was exhibited in 1877 in London at the Grosvenor Gallery. The peppery Whistler, not one to take such an assault lying down, sued for libel. In the trial that followed, Whistler explained his artistic aims and his choice of the descriptive term "Nocturne," by which he intended "to indicate an artistic interest alone in my work, divesting the picture from any outside sort of interest which might have otherwise attached to it. It is an arrangement of line, form and color first, and I make use of any incident of it which shall bring about a symmetrical result." Whistler, following Théophile Gautier's esthetic theory of *l'art pour l'art*, felt that an art object should exist for its own sake, apart from outside relationships, and should be judged a success or a failure only in terms of its internal esthetic requirements.

A century earlier Benjamin West had come to Europe and stepped into the vanguard of a revolutionary artistic movement, one concerned with man and society, and in his early paintings had anticipated French Neo-classicism by several decades. Now Whistler, another American with sensitive artistic antennae, was among the first to grasp the revolutionary implications of *l'art pour l'art*. Through his work, his philosophy of art, and indeed his eccentric life style, Whistler led the way toward modernism in art, asserting the independence of the artist and helping to establish the theoretical basis for abstract art, the most revolutionary and dynamic stylistic innovation since the development of linear perspective.

Whistler was born in Lowell, Massachusetts. Between the ages of nine and fifteen young Whistler was in Russia, where his father was consulting engineer on the railroad being built between St. Petersburg and Moscow. On the death of his father, the family returned to America where Whistler attended Pomfret Academy in Connecticut and the United States Military Academy at West Point. He compiled an unimpressive record at West Point, and was finally expelled in 1854 for "a deficiency in chemistry." Whistler then worked briefly for the government on a coastal survey, preparing drawings of the coastline and learning the craft of etching.

In 1855 Whistler went to Paris, where he enrolled in the studio of Charles Gabriel Gleyre and enthusiastically launched upon a bohemian existence which undoubtedly suited his temperament much better than the rigors of military life at West Point. In 1858-1859 he produced several superb sets of etchings of river scenes done along the Rhine and the Thames. Whistler soon treated the same themes in paintings such as *Wapping on Thames* (1861-1864, Mr. and Mrs. John Hay Whitney, New York, New York) and *The Last of Old Westminster* (1862, Museum of Fine Arts, Boston, Massachusetts). Influenced by his friend Courbet, Whistler began as an objective realist, recording the aspect and character of river life with heavy brushwork and a warm palette. In 1861 he painted *The Coast of Brittany* (Wadsworth Atheneum, Hartford, Connecticut), exhibited at the Royal Academy the following year under the title *Alone with the Tide*. The first of his major paintings of the sea, this work transcends simple realism in its emphasis on the formal juxtaposition of warm foreground tonalities of sand and rock against the cool blue of ocean and sky beyond. Whistler's drift toward more purely formal concerns is suggested in *Wapping*, as the head of his red-haired mistress Joanna Heffernan, his oft-painted Jo, re-worked as the painting progressed, reveals an abstract concern with form and color that contrasts with the realism of the other figures and the detailed background.

Jo was the model for Whistler's famous, indeed notorious, *The White Girl* (National Gallery of Art, Washington, D. C.) of 1862. A decade later, when Whistler adopted the musical terminology (Symphonies, Nocturnes, Arrangements) suggested by Baudelaire and others as better suited to his ideas of an abstract esthetic, the painting was re-titled *Symphony in White, No. 1. The White Girl* was rejected by the Royal Academy in 1862, and by the Salon in Paris the following year. Whistler therefore exhibited it at the Salon des Refusés, where it was a center of attraction along with Manet's *Déjeuner sur l'Herbe*. The daring placement of an all-white dress against a white drapery background which emphasized subtle textural modulations, the dramatic red splash of Jo's hair in a sea of white, and the tantalizing themelessness which provoked endless speculation about the "meaning" of the picture, all served and reflected Whistler's increasing preoccupation with the formal aspects of picture-making. This interest was advanced by his exposure to Japanese art. He became an active early collector of blue and white porcelain, and an admirer of Japanese color prints. Such works as *Rose and Silver: "La Princesse du Pays de la Porcelaine"* of 1864 (Freer Gallery of Art, Washington, D. C.), *Purple and Rose: The Lange Lijzen of the Six Marks* (Philadelphia Museum of Art, Philadelphia, Pennsylvania) of the same year, and the fragile *The Artist's Studio* of about 1867-1868 (Art Institute of Chicago, Chicago, Illinois) are notable among many pictures reflecting oriental attitudes toward line, perspective, subtle color relationships, and surface patterning, as well as actually introducing eastern dress. Whistler increasingly conceived of each work as a decorative entity. He designed his own molded gilt picture frames, and devised a butterfly monogram which he carefully placed on the canvas like a colophon on a Chinese or Japanese scroll, a positive element in the design.

Whistler painted his famous *Arrangement in Gray and Black No. 1: The Artist's Mother* (Louvre, Paris) in 1871. It was exhibited reluctantly the next year by the Royal Academy (Whistler never again exhibited at the Academy, and never became an Academician) and a year later at the Paris Salon. The portrait integrates the subject into a precise pattern of lines and muted color areas, devoid of any emotional involvement or sense of personality. Whistler's mother (who was something of a shrew) becomes an object among objects. The result may be impersonal, but it is a stunning picture. The painting was followed immediately by *Arrangement in Gray and Black No. 2: Thomas Carlyle* painted in 1872-1873. The famous Scottish author, philosopher, essayist and historian, who liked Whistler's portrait of his mother, is also dressed in black and silhouetted in profile against a gray background. His face, the single strong patch of color, is balanced by the rectangular shapes of pictures on the wall to the left, while Whistler's butterfly monogram perfectly completes the composition along the right edge. In addition to Whistler's almost oriental sense of design, the picture also reveals the influence of Velasquez in the restrained and harmonious color relationships. This painting, purchased by the Glasgow Corporation in 1891, was the first work by Whistler to be acquired for a public collection; immediately afterward the portrait of *The Artist's Mother* was purchased by the French government for the Luxembourg.

James Abbott McNeill Whistler (1834-1903).
Arrangement in Gray and Black No. 2: Thomas Carlyle, 1872-1873. (67⅜×56½″)
Glasgow Art Gallery and Museum, Glasgow, Scotland.

Thomas Eakins (1844-1916). The Thinker (Louis N. Kenton), 1900. (82×42″)
The Metropolitan Museum of Art, New York. Kennedy Fund, 1917.

James Abbott McNeill Whistler (1834-1903). Arrangement in Flesh Color and Black:
Portrait of Théodore Duret, 1883. (76⅛×35¾") The Metropolitan Museum of Art, New York. Wolfe Fund, 1913.

John Singer Sargent (1856-1925).
The Daughters of Edward Darley Boit, 1882. (87⅝×87⅝″) Courtesy, Museum of Fine Arts, Boston, Massachusetts.
Gift of the daughters of Edward D. Boit in memory of their father.

The uproar that greeted Whistler's nearly abstract *Nocturne in Black and Gold: The Falling Rocket* occurred at almost the same moment as the similarly outraged, but differently motivated, reaction to Eakins' realistic *Gross Clinic* in Philadelphia. Though their esthetic positions are almost diametrically opposed, Eakins and Whistler have much in common. Both were Americans, had studied in Paris, admired Courbet, and were affected by the art theories of the influential Lecoq de Boisbaudran. A comparison of Whistler's portrait of *Théodore Duret* (1882-1884) with Eakins' portrait of his brother-in-law Louis Kenton, *The Thinker* (1900), clearly shows that both were also influenced by the full-length portraits of Velasquez. Yet at the same time these two paintings and these two artists epitomize those two opposed views of art which have informed the development of modern American art.

Eakins' *Thinker* stands squarely in the American tradition of realism. Eakins is committed to reality, to the pictorial reconstruction of the real world. The subject, Kenton, is a solid mass in space modeled by light, a substantial reality that casts deep shadows. He stands in front of a wall that slants away from the picture surface to define a spatial ambient rather than to provide an abstract background. Eakins is interested in line, color, light, and other formal qualities, but not for their own sake. He does not pursue their perfection as an end, but uses them as means to achieve other pictorial goals. Yet his aim is more than the creation of an illusion of visual reality; it is more than the invocation of a mastery of anatomy to achieve an accurate and convincing impression of the physical existence of the weighty, slumping figure. Eakins has painted a man, a human being. The subject has a body, and that body contains a mind that thinks, contemplates, reflects, remembers. He has existed through time, has been weathered by experience. Eakins is more interested in this man than in art; at any rate his primary interest is not in art for its own sake but for its relevance to man and his existence.

Whistler, in his portrait of *Théodore Duret*, is more interested in the picture than in the man. He is intensely involved with the formal possibilities established by the subject; the esthetic disposition of the pattern of lights and darks, the flow of line, the exquisite harmonies of varying shades of black and halating pinks. The painting is to be judged on its internal pictorial merits, not on the fidelity of its relationship to visual reality. It is no accident that Whistler signed his picture with a butterfly monogram that floats on the surface as part of the decorative pattern, abstracting the presence of the artist into a symbol, whereas Eakins placed his actual name and the date in the lower right, tipping the signature backward through the use of perspective drawing to make it a real fact in the pictorial space. Whistler is primarily concerned with art, Eakins with reality. However just as Eakins was obviously not uninterested in the formal aspects of art, so Whistler was not uncaring about his subjects. It was simply a matter of emphasis. Duret, an art critic and early supporter of the Impressionists, and an oriental art scholar, had in fact been a close friend of Whistler's since the early 1860's, and in 1883 wrote one of the most important early biographies of the artist.

The final result of the Ruskin trial was exoneration for Whistler, who was awarded a farthing in symbolic damages, but it was a pyrrhic victory. The financial strain induced by the costs of the trial forced Whistler into bankruptcy the following year. Neither his art nor his personal fortunes ever returned to their previous heights.

Aristocratic, cultured and urbane, John Singer Sargent (1856-1924) typifies Henry James' image of the American expatriate. Whereas Whistler, born and educated in the United States, never returned to his native land, Sargent, who was born in Florence, Italy, to American parents, became increasingly involved with America in his later years. Sargent first visited the United States in 1876 at the age of twenty, having studied art briefly in Rome, and in the Paris studio of Carolus Duran. His reverse grand tour lasted for four months, and included a visit to the Centennial Exhibition in Philadelphia. On his return to Paris, Sargent began to exhibit at the Salon. During the next few years he traveled extensively through Spain, Holland and North Africa. Like Eakins he particularly admired Hals and Velasquez, and emulated their free brushwork. His earlier works, pervaded by a characteristic pearly tonality, reveal an almost impressionistic concern with atmosphere and light. The influence of Velasquez and Spain is evident in his dramatic *El Jaleo* of 1880 (Isabella Stewart Gardner Museum, Boston, Massachusetts). A row of musicians and dancers is theatrically lit, the shadowy guitarists silhouetted against a light background and a highlighted dancer against a dark setting. The figures, and the guitars hanging on the wall, are clustered like notes in a bar of music, enhancing the visual impression of music being performed. In their staccato pairings they are evocative of the flamenco rhythm, which culminates in a "bang" as the dancer slams her foot down on the floor. Subsequently the composition, in contrast to the coloristic restraint and severely ordered tempo to the left of the dancer, resolves itself into a discharge of color in the costumes of the figures at the right. Sargent was himself an accomplished pianist, and his interest in music informed certain aspects of his art, although in a more objective way than Whistler's creation of musical equivalents or Blakelock's groping on the piano keyboard for compositional inspiration.

Sargent's superb group portrait of the *Daughters of Edward Darley Boit* of 1882, exhibited at the Paris Salon the following year, is similar to *El Jaleo* in its calculated groupings and the strong value contrasts induced by the flow of light from the left creating dramatic highlights and deep pools of shadow. The color is also similarly restrained, except for the dramatic orange-red slash of the screen at the right. The careful patterning of the

Mary Cassatt (1845-1926). Little Girl in a Blue Armchair, 1878. (35×51″)
From the Collection of Mr. and Mrs. Paul Mellon, Washington, D.C.

picture surface is reminiscent of Whistler's response to Japanese prints, while the enormous blue and white Chinese vases are like wildly exaggerated Whistlerian motifs. This intimate informal view of the daughters of an artist friend gathered in the dark hallway of their Paris apartment, retrieved from the passing current of time, conveys a sense of individuals within the surroundings in which they live their lives that is more satisfying and effective in its totality than an exact delineation of each individual would be.

In 1884 Sargent exhibited his daring and controversial full-length portrait of Madame Gautreau, the painting known as Madame X (Metropolitan Museum of Art, New York, New York), at the Paris Salon. The painting is an inverse silhouette. A blast of light isolates the curving contour of the figure and the outline of the face against the background, but erases facial detail and any sense of character or personality. The picture drew biting criticism, not least of all from the sitter and her family, in part for its handling and in part for the revealing décolletage. The attack provided one of the reasons for Sargent's subsequent remove to London, where he felt his work would be more sympathetically treated.

Sargent exhibited the *Boit Children* and *El Jaleo* in Boston in 1888. His work was well received, and a few years later he was commissioned to paint murals dealing with the evolution of religion for the Boston Public Library. Later he received commissions for murals for the Boston Museum of Fine Arts and Widener Library at Harvard. During the latter decades of his life Sargent also worked increasingly with watercolor, a medium well-suited to his extraordinary technical ability. His achievements in that medium place him with Winslow Homer, Maurice Prendergast and John Marin in the top rank of American watercolorists. Despite his achievements as a muralist and watercolorist, Sargent is primarily remembered for his portraiture, particularly those overblown Edwardian full-lengths which allowed an ample arena for his extraordinary manipulative facility with the brush. Sargent's reputation suffers to some extent from that very facility which has obscured the fact that many of his portraits reflect an awareness of human personality that, if not as probing as Eakins, goes well beyond the mere surface replication of appearances. And more profound images, such as the memorable *Gassed* (London War Museum, London), perhaps the most striking picture to come out of World War I, suggest the achievement of which Sargent was capable but only infrequently attained.

The third member of what may be conveniently considered as the expatriate triumvirate (as opposed to a native trinity of Homer, Eakins and Ryder) was Mary Cassatt (1845-1926). The most significant American female artist prior to the twentieth century, Mary Cassatt was born near Pittsburgh, Pennsylvania. Much of her childhood was spent abroad, but she received some early art training at the Pennsylvania Academy of Fine Arts in Philadelphia in 1864-1865, where she may well have been a fellow student of young Eakins. She later studied in Paris and in Parma at the academy of Carlo Raimondi, and traveled extensively throughout Spain and the Low Countries. Like so many artists in the second half of the nineteenth century, she was influenced by Hals and the great Spanish seventeenth century masters, and her early work reflects this in its dark colors and fluid brushwork. A friend of Degas, she began to exhibit with the Impressionists in the late 1870's. Under the influence of the Impressionists, her palette lightened, but her color remained assertive, and she relied heavily on texture and modeling for her effects. *Woman and Child Driving* of 1881 (Philadelphia Museum of Art, Philadelphia, Pennsylvania), depicting her sister Lydia and Degas' niece in a carriage, is clearly influenced by Degas both in subject and the arbitrary composition. When Eakins painted his contemporaneous and thematically similar *Fairman Rogers' Four-in-Hand*, he strove to attain an anatomically correct disposition of limbs in representing animal locomotion, and requested that the carriage be driven past him again and again in order to study the subject. Mary Cassatt, by contrast, devoted her attention to the design of the picture, caring little for anatomy or locomotion. Indeed, like Degas, she does not hesitate arbitrarily to trim off parts of the horse and carriage in order to achieve an effective composition.

The Little Girl in a Blue Armchair of 1878 reflects the same dominance of pictorial concern. The viewer's forcibly depressed line of vision eliminates the ceiling and much of the far wall, while the floor slopes up and almost reaches the upper framing edge of the picture. The windows and upholstered chairs are arbitrarily cut by the frame to form pleasing new shapes. The curving recession of the chairs diagonally to the left and the compressed space echo an arrangement familiar from Degas' ballet interiors. The picture is coloristically firm, and a variety of textured patterns enliven the surface. The painting seems to combine Degas' sense of space and composition, Renoir's color and Manet's assertive forms into an effective synthesis that marks Mary Cassatt's early style at its best.

During the 1880's Cassatt's style did not change markedly. However in 1890 she went with Degas to see the great exhibition of Japanese prints in Paris, which profoundly influenced her subsequent work. The following year she produced a set of ten colored prints in dry-point and aquatint, very Japanese in their sense of line and the careful arrangement of flat color areas, that are among the most beautiful works of graphic art ever produced by an American artist. The theme of mother and child began to dominate her work after 1890. One of her most effective paintings on the maternal theme is *The Bath* (c. 1891, Art Institute of Chicago, Chicago, Illinois), in which the figures are viewed sharply from above, creating an unexpected disposition of color areas on the picture surface that is extraordinarily Japanese in character. Less subtle, but more dramatic coloristically, is *The Boating Party* (National Gallery of Art, Washington, D. C.) in which, apparently under the influence of the Post-Impressionists, notably Gauguin, Cassatt divides the surface into broad flat areas of brilliant primary blue and yellow. The arbitrary viewpoint again raises the horizon line to

William Merritt Chase (1849-1916). In the Studio, about 1880 (?). (28½×40¼″)
The Brooklyn Museum, Brooklyn, New York. Gift of Mrs. C.H. DeSilver.

Childe Hassam (1859-1935). Rainy Day, Rue Bonaparte, Paris, 1887. (40¼×77¼″)
Harry Spiro Collection, New York.

the top of the canvas, resulting in an inescapable emphasis upon the design. The maternal theme is present, although overwhelmed by the striking visual context. The relentless emphasis upon its formal aspects removes this picture a substantial distance from such antecedents as Mount's *Eel Spearing at Setauket* or Homer's *Fog Warning*.

Another American artist who enjoyed a direct link with a major French Impressionist was Theodore Robinson (1852-1896), who knew and worked with Claude Monet briefly at Giverny. However Robinson was not robust, and died prematurely without exerting much impact on American painting. Much more active and influential in transmitting aspects of Impressionist painting to America was William Merritt Chase (1849-1916) who, after his initial training in Munich, abandoned the dark palette of that school for the brighter colors of French Impressionism, which he applied, as in his impressive *In the Studio*, with facile brushstrokes in the manner of John Singer Sargent. An influential teacher after his return to America, Chase communicated a largely derivative emphasis on technical facility and rapid brushwork to many budding American artists.

A more distinctively American brand of Impressionism did develop, however, which occasionally led to remarkable, still under-appreciated, pictorial achievements. One of the best known, although not the most original, of the American Impressionists was Childe Hassam (1859-1935). Hassam was raised in the vicinity of Boston, and began his career with a number of remarkable scenes of city streets infused with moody atmospheric effects of rain, snow or twilight revealing Hassam's roots in the tradition of American Luminism. When he went to Paris in 1886, Hassam became aware of the innovations of the French Impressionists, especially Monet, Pissarro and Sisley. His large canvas of 1887, *Une Averse, La Rue Bonaparte*, marks the moment when the sensitivity to place and atmosphere that characterized his earlier American work was first informed by an Impressionist sense of color to produce an especially happy result.

John H. Twachtman (1853-1902). The White Bridge. (30¼×20¼″)
The Minneapolis Institute of Arts, Minneapolis, Minnesota. Martin B. Koon Memorial Collection.

Hassam's early city scenes almost invariably contain, as here, a deep perspective thrust into pictorial space, reminiscent of major paintings by Bingham or early Homer. However an important characteristic of American Impressionism is the replacement of this spatial concern by a commitment to the picture surface. Although American Impressionism derived from French Impressionism, it developed considerably later and was therefore also affected by Post-Impressionism, Art Nouveau, and eventually Neo-Impressionism. By virtue of its unrelieved concern with the decorative quality of the picture surface and its muted and restrained palette, American Impressionism is immediately recognizable as something different and distinct from its French counterpart.

A case in point is John H. Twachtman's *The White Bridge*. Twachtman (1853-1902) was one of the most gifted and sensitive American Impressionists, still not adequately esteemed in his own country. With rare exceptions, such as the sensitive and perceptive collector Duncan Phillips who acquired and hung paintings by Twachtman in the company of major French Impressionist works, few recognized the validity and importance of Twachtman's accomplishment. The true nature of his subtle art was perceptively described by Edgar P. Richardson who noted that it was more akin to French Impressionist music than painting. Twachtman disposes pools of color on the picture surface in writhing irregular shapes, and weaves a delicate tracery of lines into an "all-over" surface pattern that anticipates mid-twentieth century abstract art.

A group of American artists who can more or less be classified as Impressionists exhibited together in 1895 as the Ten American Painters. Hassam and Twachtman belonged to The Ten, as did J. Alden Weir (1852-1919). Weir came from a distinguished family of American painters. His father, Robert W. Weir (1803-1889), was professor of drawing at West Point (where he taught Whistler) for many years, and his brother, John Ferguson Weir, was a successful artist and the first director of the Yale School of Fine Arts. J. Alden Weir's brand of Impressionism was slightly bolder than Twachtman's, but embodied the same primary orientation toward overall decorative treatment of the picture surface. His

J. Alden Weir (1852-1919). The Red Bridge. (24¼×33¾")
The Metropolitan Museum of Art, New York. Gift of Mrs. John A. Rutherford, 1914.

Maurice Prendergast (1859-1924). Ponte della Paglia, Venice, 1899. (28×23″)
The Phillips Collection, Washington, D.C.

painting *The Red Bridge*, with its subtle and effective use of color, stands as one of the high points of American Impressionism. The flanking foreground trees, recalling a standard landscape device, are used here not so much to frame the composition as to complete the design with their sinuous movement.

For more than a century, from the time of Whistler to the present, a rapid succession of artistic developments have been powered by the liberating concept that an art object exists for the sake of art. Indeed, it is difficult to determine on other than strictly chronological grounds where to draw the line between nineteenth and twentieth century art. But if one had to find that moment in the history of American art, it might well occur in the work of Maurice Prendergast. Prendergast's *Ponte della Paglia* of 1899 combines the commitment to the picture surface that informs the work of American Impressionists with a more highly developed interest in pure color. Prendergast, whose delight in blobs of color manifested itself in a fascination with balloons, parasols and banners, shared that immersion in problems of color and color theory that marked the growth of western art during the last decade of the nineteenth century and the first two decades of the twentieth. Influenced by Vuillard and such arcane sources as Persian miniatures, Prendergast returned time and again, especially in his late oils, to the bold textural and coloristic surface effects found in the early *Ponte della Paglia*. As is evident in his *Central Park* of 1901, he was also one of the most gifted of all American watercolorists. His touches of limpid watercolor provide the viewer with a pure sensual delight not often found in American painting which, perhaps as the result of a Puritan heritage and a tradition of pragmatism, tends to pursue more serious ends.

Maurice Prendergast (1859-1924). Central Park, 1901. (14⅛×21¾″)
Pencil and Watercolor. Collection Whitney Museum of American Art, New York.

William Glackens (1870-1938) was another artist sensitive to developments in European art, especially in the realm of color. However he was simultaneously deeply involved with an important indigenous movement as a member of a vital group of artists that matured in Philadelphia during the last decade of the nineteenth century. This group, which also included John Sloan (1871-1951), George Luks (1867-1933), Everett Shinn (1876-1953), and Robert Henri (1865-1929), was to a greater or lesser extent in each case, influenced by Thomas Anshutz, who had succeeded Eakins as Professor of Drawing and Painting at the Pennsylvania Academy of Fine Arts. Anshutz conveyed to these young artists the Eakins tradition of art involved with life. Many of them began as journalists, producing illustrations for the *Philadelphia Press*. By the turn of the century they had all settled in New York. Glackens, although he shared the same background and orientation as the others, was atypical in his pronounced, if conservative, sensitivity to French painting. Gifted with an innate sense of color, Glackens, like Prendergast, produced paintings that are sources of visual delight rather than transmitters of messages. His early *Hammerstein's Roof Garden* of circa 1901 has an almost Whistlerian delicacy. Formal qualities of composition and color seem more important than the people or the event depicted. In subsequent paintings, such as his popular *Chez Mouquin* (1905, Art Institute of Chicago), Glackens was clearly influenced by Renoir, the greatest of all impressionist colorists. Indeed Glackens' affinity for Renoir is so pronounced that he is sometimes dismissed as a follower. However when his best work is seen in depth, as in the splendid collection in Philadelphia assembled by the artist's friend Dr. Albert C. Barnes, it is evident that Glackens may have been the most gifted painter of his whole circle.

The leader of the young artists who moved from Philadelphia to New York, although not the best painter among them, was Robert Henri. Senior in years and inspiring in person, Henri was the theoretician who gave voice and direction to the artistic concerns of the group in his influential book, *The Art Spirit*, infusing the realistic tradition of Eakins with new force and relevance. An admirer of Hals, Velasquez and Manet for their spirited brushwork which enabled them to record their perceptions with immediacy and verve, Henri's concept of painting as a means for a bold personal response to the real world stood diametrically opposed to the delicate estheticism of most American Impressionists, artists like The Ten, who worked in the "genteel tradition" during the closing years of the nineteenth century. Not all of the artists who admired Henri followed his teaching in their own practice. Glackens, for example, was much more concerned with pictorial effects, as were Prendergast and Shinn. But Sloan and Luks were active practitioners of Henri's brand of Realism—a Realism attuned to early twentieth century life.

A generation earlier, Homer and Eakins had carried American Realism to new heights. Taking as their point of departure the realistic genre scenes of Mount and Bingham, they had divested their realism of sentiment or narrative frosting, and offered reality alone, albeit structured, ordered and carefully selected reality. Homer concerned himself almost exclusively with non-urban life, while Eakins, although deeply involved in the life of the city himself, depicted rivers and marshes, or interior scenes that effectively conveyed no sense of an urban setting. Moreover, their images were fixed and static. Eakins, for example, strove for a distillation of the essence of the scene depicted. The younger artists, led by Henri, wanted to get much closer to the reality of life in their own time. They wanted to capture in their art the actual sensory feel of existence, the "spirit" of contemporary life. They wanted to be where the action was, and the action was in the city. These artists, for the first time in the history of American art, chose to paint the city, and did not restrict themselves to pleasing aspects of urban life. Impelled by a journalistic instinct to get at the truth, they, like such contemporary naturalist writers as Theodore Dreiser and Frank Norris, looked with fresh eyes at the realities of man and his world, and recorded what they saw. Often their paintings were charged with social consciousness. For example, few previous artists had dealt bluntly with the subject of man and his work. Early portraiture had occasionally

William Glackens (1870-1938). Hammerstein's Roof Garden, about 1901. (30×25″)
Collection Whitney Museum of American Art, New York.

hinted at this aspect of a man's life by introducing some element of the sitter's occupation into the decor—a desk, a Bible, a ship in the background. Neagle's *Pat Lyon at the Forge* anticipated mid-nineteenth century genre scenes by showing the subject within the context of his occupation. However Bingham's paintings of river life or Mount's farm scenes invariably represented the more leisurely and pleasant aspects of work. Eakins, in the *Gross Clinic*, made a daring move into new ground by opening up unpleasant parts of a man's

George Luks (1867-1933). The Miner. (60×51″)
National Gallery of Art, Washington, D.C. Gift of Chester Dale.

George Bellows (1882-1925). Both Members of This Club, 1909. (45¼×63⅛″)
National Gallery of Art, Washington, D.C. Gift of Chester Dale.

work as acceptable subject matter. In *The Miner* George Luks went a step further toward an immediate, direct visual report and social commentary. The miner, after a day of hard physical labor, sits covered with soot. His bulky figure sags from exhaustion. Sapped of energy, his muscles can barely counteract the downward pull of gravity. Depression and exhaustion pervade this somber image. There is nothing in the theme or its treatment to evoke pleasure. This is a grim message of truth about one man's world, and there is an implicit point that the miner's lot should be improved.

In 1907 a group of paintings by Luks, Sloan and Glackens were rejected for exhibition by the National Academy of Design. Henri, an academician, withdrew his own pictures in protest. The following year these artists, along with Shinn, Prendergast, Ernest Lawson (1873-1939) and Arthur B. Davies (1862-1928), exhibited as a group, subsequently known as The Eight, at the Macbeth Gallery in New York. The Eight were by no means artistically homogeneous. Their work ranged from the realism of Henri, Sloan and Luks through the French-influenced paintings of Glackens, Shinn, Prendergast and Lawson to imaginative idylls by Arthur B. Davies that represented a late phase of the "genteel tradition." Although these artists never exhibited again as a group, the long-range impact of their one show was considerable. Despite their varying degrees of involvement with "modernism," The Eight stood together in openness toward new directions in art and a desire for

John Sloan (1871-1951). The Wake of the Ferry, 1907. (26×32″)
The Phillips Collection, Washington, D.C.

independence from the once revolutionary but now calcified National Academy of Design. At the exhibition, the realistic pictures of Sloan, Luks and to a lesser extent Henri, which celebrated the confusion of noise, dirt and smells of city life, the complicated mixture of people and customs that gives character to the urban environment, drew the most critical attention and scorn. As a result the entire group was tagged with the sobriquet "Ashcan School." These artists were imbued with a sense of artistic mission, to tell it like it is, and younger artists, like George Bellows (1882-1925), flocked to the banner of the Ashcan School. Bellows studied with Henri, and inspired by his teaching, began to produce vivid city scenes. Bellows also seems consciously to have chosen some themes treated earlier by Eakins, altering their character by emphasizing action rather than stability. For example, his *Forty-two Kids* of 1907 (Corcoran Gallery of Art, Washington, D. C.) is a frenetic variation on the theme of Eakins' *The Swimming Hole*. His boxing scenes such as *Both Members of This Club* of 1909 echo Eakins' boxing scenes, but whereas Eakins sought the synthetic moment of stability, Bellows asserted movement, change, flux. The two boxers, one black and one white, are locked in combat, drawing blood from each other and roars from the crowd. A row of heads in the foreground sets the stage for the action, putting the viewer in the audience where he can almost hear the roar and smell the smoke and the people, as he perceives the "feel" of the event. When a critic objected that Bellows had not depicted accurately the positions in which boxers hold their hands and plant their feet, Bellows replied: "I don't know anything about boxing. I am just painting two men trying to kill each other."

The young American painters were proud of their achievement. They had taken a brand of realism that was in the mainstream of traditional American art, and had moved it into new, adventurous and exciting ground. Their art, as in John Sloan's evocation of the ferry ride between Manhattan Island and Jersey City in his powerful *Wake of the Ferry* of 1907, dealt with real life and real people. It was democratic art, depicting not the aristocratic classes who populated the paintings of the "genteel tradition," but the lower middle classes, the great mass of the American populace. Their sense of artistic purpose was heightened by the fact that existing institutions for the education and encouragement of young artists such as the National Academy of Design, the places where art was exhibited and artists made contact with potential patrons, had become rigid and conservative, providing an authority against which to rebel, an enemy to fight. The young American artists were anxious to show off their art to their fellow Americans, sure that an appreciative public would give them the patronage they required. To this end they decided to hold a large independent exhibition in 1913, the exhibition that has become famous as the Armory Show, probably the most important single event in the history of American art.

In order to flesh out their undertaking, the Americans decided to include work by European contemporaries in the exhibition. They were anxious to prove that the novelty of their art was not eccentric or parochial, but part of a general wave of modernism throughout the world. The local manifestation was seen as a leading accomplishment of the new spirit that was liberating all art, something of which Americans could and should be proud. The major figure behind the Armory Show was the aristocratic Arthur B. Davies, a charter member of The Eight, but whose real interests, despite the deceptive conservatism of his own work, lay in the direction of European modernism. Approximately one third of the 1500 objects in the enormous exhibition were European works. The Armory Show opened in New York on February 17, 1913. As the American public gradually awoke to the existence of the show, it reacted violently. However the reaction was not against the works of the young American realists, who were ignored, but against the more advanced European works, notably those of Matisse and Marcel Duchamp, whose *Nude descending the Staircase* (Philadelphia Museum of Art, Philadelphia, Pennsylvania) became a symbol of the exhibition. American artists may have thought that the works of Ashcan painters like Luks, Sloan, or Bellows (who actually hung the exhibition) were novel and exciting in their realistic views of urban life, but when Bellows' boxers or Luks' city scenes were compared with a European-influenced abstraction such as Joseph Stella's *Coney Island*, the new realism suddenly seemed old hat and tame.

The ghost of Whistler and the doctrine of art for art's sake had returned in the form of abstract art, and the realist tradition in American painting would never recover from the shock of this confrontation. Although the public reviled modernism and abstraction, and made fun of Matisse and Duchamp, many of the younger American artists quickly became aware of the importance of what they saw at the Armory Show, realizing that here was a quicker and more exhilarating path to artistic independence. The battle between realism and abstraction was joined, and the ebb and flow of the contest has marked the history of American art ever since.

Select Bibliography

General Index

Select Bibliography

SOURCE WORKS

The most important general reference work for American art is GEORGE C. GROCE and DAVID H. WALLACE, *The New-York Historical Society's Dictionary of Artists in America, 1564-1860* (New Haven and London, 1957). This supersedes for the period prior to the Civil War such earlier compendia as RALPH CLIFTON SMITH's *Biographical Index of American Artists* (Baltimore, 1930) and MANTLE FIELDING's *Dictionary of American Painters, Sculptors and Engravers* (Philadelphia, 1926). — Useful information can be found in many biographical dictionaries, among which the *Dictionary of American Biography* and ULRICH THIEME and FELIX BECKER's *Allgemeines Lexikon der bildenden Künstler* stand out as the most useful. — The most comprehensive bibliography for the field is again found in GROCE and WALLACE's *Dictionary of American Artists*. — A valuable earlier effort is ELIZABETH MCCAUSLAND's "A Selected Bibliography on American Painting and Sculpture from Colonial Times to the Present," *Magazine of Art* (November, 1946), pp. 329-349. — An especially good annotated bibliography of American art literature in terms of its relevance for the study of American history is WENDELL D. GARRETT and JANE N. GARRETT's "A Bibliography of the Arts in Early American History," *The Arts in American History* (Chapel Hill, 1965), pp. 35-170. — The *Art Index* is an essential guide to the periodical literature since 1929. Access to earlier material is more difficult, but Poole's *Index to Periodical Literature* (1802-1906) and GRIFFIN's *Writings in American History* (1906-1940) are useful. A number of twentieth century periodicals have concentrated on American art, especially *Antiques* (1922-   ), *Art in America* (1913-   ), and *Art Quarterly* (1938-   ).

GENERAL WORKS

Armory Show Fiftieth Anniversary Exhibition, Munson-Williams-Proctor Institute, Utica, and Armory of the Sixty-ninth Regiment, New York, 1963. — VIRGIL BARKER, *American Painting, History and Interpretation*, New York, 1950. — JOHN I. H. BAUR, *Revolution and Tradition in Modern American Art*, Cambridge, 1951. — FRANK W. BAYLEY, *Five Colonial Artists of New England*, Boston, 1929. — WALDRON PHOENIX BELKNAP, Jr., *American Painting: Materials for a History*, Cambridge, 1959. — SAMUEL GREENE WHEELER BENJAMIN, *Art in America: A Critical and Historical Sketch*, New York, 1880. — Idem, *Fifty Years of American Art, 1828-1878*, Harper's New Monthly Magazine LIX, July, 1879, pp. 241-257; Sept. 1879, pp. 481-496; Oct. 1879, pp. 673-688. — Idem, *Our American Artists*, Boston, 1879. — YVON BIZARDEL, *American Painters in Paris*, New York, 1960. — MARY BLACK and JEAN LIPMAN, *American Folk Painting*, New York, 1966. — EDWIN BEACH BLASHFIELD, *Mural Painting in America*, New York, 1913. — THEODORE BOLTON, *Early American Portrait Draughtsmen in Crayons*, New York, 1923. — Idem, *Early American Portrait Painters in Miniature*, New York, 1921. — WOLFGANG BORN, *American Landscape Painting; an Interpretation*, New Haven, 1948. — Idem, *Still-Life Painting in America*, New York, 1947. — MILTON W. BROWN, *The Story of the Armory Show*, New York, 1963. — ALAN BURROUGHS, *Limners and Likenesses: Three Centuries of American Painting*, Cambridge, 1936. — CHARLES H. CAFFIN, *American Masters of Painting*, New York, 1902. — Idem, *The Story of American Painting*, New York, 1907. — JAMES T. CALLOW, *Kindred Spirits: Knickerbocker Writers and American Artists, 1807-1855*, Chapel Hill, 1967. — BENJAMIN CHAMPNEY, *Sixty Years' Memories of Art and Artists*, Woburn (Mass.), 1900. — ELIOT CLARK, *History of the National Academy of Design, 1825-1953*, New York, 1954. — ROYAL CORTISSOZ, *American Artists*, New York and London, 1923. — MARY BARTLETT COWDREY, *American Academy of Fine Arts and American Art-Union*, New York, 1953. — Idem, *National Academy of Design Exhibition Record, 1826-1860*, New York, 1943. — THOMAS S. CUMMINGS, *Historic Annals of the National Academy of Design*, Philadelphia, 1865. — MARSHALL B. DAVIDSON, *Life in America*, Boston, 1951. — HAROLD E. DICKSON, *Arts of the Young Republic*, Chapel Hill, 1969. — Idem, ed., *Observations on American Art: Selections from the Writings of John Neal*, State College (Pa.), 1943. — LOUISA

DRESSER, ed., *XVIIth Century Painting in New England*, Worcester (Mass.), 1935. — WILLIAM DUNLAP, *Diary of William Dunlap (1766-1839)*, ed. by Dorothy C. Barck, New York, 1930. — Idem, *History of the Rise and Progress of the Arts of Design in the United States*, 2 vols., New York, 1834. — Idem, *History of the Rise and Progress of the Arts of Design in the United States*, ed. by Frank W. Bayley and Charles E. Goodspeed, 3 vols., Boston, 1918. — Idem, *History of the Rise and Progress of the Arts of Design in the United States*, Introduction by William Campbell, ed. by Alexander Wyckoff, 3 vols., New York, 1965. — ALEXANDER ELIOT, *Three Hundred Years of American Painting*, New York, 1957. — CHARLES E. FAIRMAN, *Art and Artists of the Capitol of the United States of America*, Washington, 1927. — JAMES T. FLEXNER, *America's Old Masters: First Artists of the New World*, New York, 1939. — Idem, *First Flowers of our Wilderness*, Boston, 1947. — Idem, *The Light of Distant Skies, 1760-1835*, New York, 1954. — Idem, *The Pocket History of American Painting*, New York, 1962. — Idem, *That Wilder Image*, New York, 1962. — ALFRED V. FRANKENSTEIN, *After the Hunt: William Harnett and Other American Still-life Painters, 1870-1900*, Berkeley and Los Angeles, 1963. — ALBERT TENEYCK GARDNER and STUART P. FELD, *American Paintings*, New York, 1965. — SAMUEL M. GREEN, *American Art: A Historical Survey*, New York, 1966. — GEORGE C. GROCE, *New York Painting Before 1800*, New York History XIX, Jan. 1938, pp. 44-57. — OSKAR HAGEN, *The Birth of the American Tradition in Art*, New York and London, 1940. — NEIL HARRIS, *The Artist in American Society: the Formative Years 1790-1860*, New York, 1966. — SADAKICHI HARTMANN, *The History of American Art*, 2 vols., Boston, 1902. — ELLEN W. HENDERSON, *The Pennsylvania Academy of the Fine Arts and Other Collections of Philadelphia*, Boston, 1911. — SAMUEL ISHAM, *The History of American Painting*, New York, 1905. — *M. and M. Karolik Collection of American Paintings, 1815-1865*, Cambridge, 1949. — WILLIAM KELBY, *Notes on American Artists 1754-1820*, New York, 1922. — SUZANNE LAFOLLETTE, *Art in America*, New York and London, 1929. — OLIVER W. LARKIN, *Art and Life in America*, New York, 1960 (first edition 1949). — CHARLES E. LESTER, *The Artists of America*, New York, 1846. — *Life in America*, Metropolitan Museum of Art, New York, 1939. — JEAN LIPMAN, *American Primitive Painting*, New York, 1942. — Idem, *What is American in American Art*, New York, 1963. — Idem and ALICE WINCHESTER, *Primitive Painters in America 1750-1850*, New York, 1950. — NINA FLETCHER LITTLE, *American Decorative Wall Painting 1700-1850*, Sturbridge (Mass.), 1952. — STEFAN LORANT, *The New World*, New York, 1946. — JOHN W. McCOUBREY, *American Tradition in Painting*, New York, 1963. — Idem, *Painting*, The Arts in America: the Colonial Period, New York, 1966, pp. 149-249. — Idem, *American Art, 1700-1960: Sources and Documents*, Englewood Cliffs (N.J.), 1965. — HAROLD McCRACKEN, *Portrait of the Old West*, New York, Toronto and London, 1952. — RICHARD B. McLANATHAN, *The American Tradition in the Arts*, New York, 1968. — J. WALKER McSPADDEN, *Famous Painters of America*, New York, 1923. — FRANK JEWETT MATHER, Jr., CHARLES RUFUS MOREY, and WILLIAM JAMES HENDERSON, *The American Spirit in Art*, vol. XII, The Pageant of America, New Haven, 1927. — JEROME MELLQUIST,

The Emergence of an American Art, New York, 1942. — DANIEL M. MENDELOWITZ, *A History of American Art*, New York, 1960. — LILLIAN B. MILLER, *Patrons and Patriotism: the Encouragement of the Fine Arts in the United States 1790-1860*, Chicago and London, 1966. — EUGEN NEUHAUS, *The History and Ideals of American Art*, Stanford (Cal.), 1931. — *New England Miniatures 1750-1850*, compiled and edited by Barbara N. Parker, Museum of Fine Arts, Boston, 1957. — REMBRANDT PEALE, *Reminiscences*, The Crayon I-III, 1855-1856. — BERNARD B. PERLMAN, *The Immortal Eight: American Painting from Eakins to the Armory Show*, New York, 1962. — WILLIAM H. PIERSON, JR., and MARTHA DAVIDSON, ed., *Arts of the United States: a Pictorial Survey*, New York, Toronto and London, 1960. — J. HALL PLEASANTS, *Four Late Eighteenth Century Anglo-American Landscape Painters*, Proceedings of the American Antiquarian Society LII, Oct. 1942, pp. 187-324. — EDGAR P. RICHARDSON, *American Romantic Painting*, New York, 1944. — Idem, *Painting in America: The Story of 450 Years*, New York, 1956. — Idem, *A Short History of Painting in America: The Story of 450 Years*, New York, 1963 (an abridgement of the previous item, with some new material). — BARBARA ROSE, *American Art Since 1900: A Critical History*, New York and Washington, 1967. — Idem, ed. *Readings in American Art Since 1900: A Documentary Survey*, New York and Washington, 1968. — HENRY P. ROSSITER, *M. and M. Karolik Collection of American Watercolors & Drawings, 1800-1875*, 2 vols., Boston, 1962. — ANNA WELLS RUTLEDGE, *Cumulative Record of Exhibition Catalogues, The Pennsylvania Academy of the Fine Arts, 1807-1870, The Society of Artists, 1800-1814, The Artists' Fund Society, 1835-1845*, American Philosophical Society Memoirs XXXVIII, Philadelphia, 1955. — HOMER SAINT-GAUDENS, *The American Artist and His Times*, New York, 1941. — JOHN SARTAIN, *The Reminiscences of a Very Old Man 1808-1897*, New York, 1899. — CLARA E. SEARS, *Highlights Among the Hudson River Artists*, Boston, 1947. — Idem, *Some American Primitives*, Boston, 1941. — GEORGE W. SHELDON, *American Painters*, New York, 1879. — Idem, *Recent Ideals of American Art*, 8 vols., New York and London, 1888. — JAMES THRALL SOBY and DOROTHY C. MILLER, *Romantic Painting in America*, New York, 1943. — THOMAS SULLY, *Recollections of an Old Painter*, Hours at Home X, Philadelphia, 1873, p. 69 ff. — PAVEL PETROVICH SVIN'IN, *Picturesque United States of America 1811-1813*, ed. by Abraham Yarmolinsky, New York, 1930. — MABEL M. SWAN, *The Athenaeum Gallery 1827-1873*, Boston, 1940. — FREDERICK A. SWEET, *The Hudson River School and the Early American Landscape Tradition*, Chicago, 1945. — THOMAS BANGS THORPE, *New York Artists Fifty Years Ago*, Appleton's Journal VII, May 25, 1872. — HENRY T. TUCKERMAN, *Artist-Life: or Sketches of American Painters*, New York and Philadelphia, 1847. — Idem, *Book of the Artists*, New York and London, 1867. — JOHN WALKER and MACGILL JAMES, *Great American Paintings from Smibert to Bellows, 1729-1924*, New York, 1943. — HARRY B. WEHLE and THEODORE BOLTON, *American Miniatures 1738-1850*, New York, 1927. — JOHN FERGUSON WEIR, *The Recollections of John Ferguson Weir 1869-1913*, ed. by Theodore Sizer, New York and New Haven, 1957. — JOHN WILMERDING, *A History of American Marine Painting*, Boston and Toronto, 1968.

INDIVIDUAL ARTISTS

Washington Allston: JARED B. FLAGG, *The Life and Letters of Washington Allston*, New York, 1892. — EDGAR P. RICHARDSON, *Washington Allston: A Study of the Romantic Artist in America*, Chicago, 1948.

Ezra Ames: THEODORE BOLTON and IRWIN F. CORTELYOU, *Ezra Ames of Albany... 1768-1836*, New York, 1955.

Joseph Badger: LAWRENCE PARK, *An Account of Joseph Badger, and a Descriptive List of His Work*, Proceedings of the Massachusetts Historical Society LI, Dec. 1917, pp. 158-201. — LAWRENCE PARK, *Joseph Badger of Boston, and His Portraits of Children*, Old-Time New England XIII, Jan. 1923, pp. 99-109.

George Bellows: CHARLES H. MORGAN, *George Bellows*, New York, 1965.

George Caleb Bingham: E. MAURICE BLOCH, *George Caleb Bingham*, 2 vols., Berkeley and Los Angeles, 1967. — ALBERT CHRIST-JANER, *George Caleb Bingham of Missouri*, New York, 1940. — JOHN FRANCIS MCDERMOTT, *George Caleb Bingham*, Norman (Okla.), 1959.

Joseph Blackburn: LAWRENCE PARK, *Joseph Blackburn, Colonial Portrait Painter, with a Descriptive List of His Works*, Worcester (Mass.), 1923. — JOHN HILL MORGAN and HENRY WILDER FOOTE, *An Extension of Lawrence Park's Descriptive List of the Work of Joseph Blackburn*, Worcester (Mass.), 1937.

David G. Blythe: DOROTHY MILLER, *The Life and Work of David G. Blythe*, Pittsburgh, 1950.

Mary Cassatt: FREDERICK A. SWEET, *Miss Mary Cassatt, Impressionist from Pennsylvania*, Norman (Okla.), 1966.

George Catlin: LOYD HABERLY, *Pursuit of the Horizon: The Life of George Catlin*, New York, 1948.

Frederic Church: DAVID C. HUNTINGTON, *The Landscapes of Frederic Edwin Church: Vision of an American Era*, New York, 1966.

Thomas Cole: EVERETT PARKER LESLEY, *Thomas Cole and the Romantic Sensibility*, Art Quarterly V, Summer 1942, pp. 199-220. — LOUIS L. NOBLE, *The Course of Empire, Voyage of Life, and Other Pictures of Thomas Cole, N.A., with Selections from His Letters and Miscellaneous Writings, Illustrative of His Life, Character and Genius*, New York, 1853 (revised edition by Elliot S. Vesell, *The Life and Works of Thomas Cole*, Cambridge, 1964).

John Singleton Copley: MARTHA BABCOCK AMORY, *Domestic and Artistic Life of John Singleton Copley, R.A.*, Boston, 1882. — FRANK W. BAYLEY, *The Life and Works of John Singleton Copley*, Boston, 1915. — JAMES T. FLEXNER, *John Singleton Copley*, Boston, 1948. *Letters and Papers of John Singleton Copley and Henry Pelham, 1739-1776*, ed. by Charles Francis Adams, II, Guernsey Jones, and Worthington Chauncey Ford, Massachusetts Historical Society Collections LXXI, Boston, 1914. — BARBARA N. PARKER and ANNE B. WHEELER, *John Singleton Copley*, Boston, 1938. — AUGUSTUS T. PERKINS, *A Sketch of the Life and a List of Some of the Works of John Singleton Copley*, Boston, 1873. — JULES DAVID PROWN, *John Singleton Copley*, 2 vols., Cambridge, 1966; idem, *John Singleton Copley*, Catalogue of Exhibition at the National Gallery of Art, Metropolitan Museum of Art, and the Museum of Fine Arts, Boston, 1965-1966.

William Dunlap: ORAL SUMNER COAD, *William Dunlap, a Study of His Life and Works and of His Place in Contemporary Culture*, New York, 1917.

Asher B. Durand: JOHN DURAND, *The Life and Times of A. B. Durand*, New York, 1894.

Thomas Eakins: LLOYD GOODRICH, *Thomas Eakins: His Life and Work*, New York, 1933. Fairfield Porter, *Thomas Eakins*, New York, 1959.

Ralph Earl: LAURENCE B. GOODRICH, *Ralph Earl: Recorder for an Era*, Albany (N.Y.), 1967. WILLIAM SAWITZKY, *Ralph Earl, 1751-1801*, New York and Worcester 1945.

Louis M. Eilshemius: WILLIAM SCHACK, *And He Sat Among the Ashes*, New York, 1939.

Charles Fraser: ALICE R. H. SMITH and D. E. H. SMITH, *Charles Fraser*, New York, 1924.

Robert Feke: HENRY WILDER FOOTE, *Robert Feke: Colonial Portrait Painter*, Cambridge, 1930.

William Glackens: IRA GLACKENS, *William Glackens and the Ashcan Group*, New York, 1957.

John Greenwood: ALAN BURROUGHS, *John Greenwood in America, 1745-1752: a Monograph with Notes and a Checklist*, Andover (Mass.), 1943.

Chester Harding: CHESTER HARDING, *My Egotistography*, Boston, 1866.

Childe Hassam: ADELINE ADAMS, *Childe Hassam*, New York, 1938.

Martin Johnson Heade: ROBERT G. MCINTYRE, *Martin Johnson Heade*, New York, 1948.

George P. A. Healy: MADELINE CHARLES BIGOT, *Life of George P. A. Healy*, Chicago, 1913. — MARIE DE MARE, *G. P. A. Healy, American Artist*, New York, 1954. — GEORGE P. A. HEALY, *Reminiscences of a Portrait Painter*, Chicago, 1894.

Robert Henri: ROBERT HENRI, *The Art Spirit*, New York, 1923; new edition by Margery A. Ryerson, Philadelphia and New York, 1960. — HELEN APPLETON READ, *Robert Henri*, New York, 1931.

Edward L. Henry: ELIZABETH MCCAUSLAND, *The Life and Work of Edward Lamson Henry, N.A., 1841-1919*, New York, 1945.

Edward Hicks: ALICE FORD, *Edward Hicks, Painter of the Peaceable Kingdom*, Philadelphia, 1952.

Winslow Homer: PHILIP C. BEAM, *Winslow Homer at Prout's Neck*, Boston and Toronto, 1966. — WILLIAM HOWE DOWNES, *The Life and Works of Winslow Homer*, Boston, 1911. — JAMES T. FLEXNER and the Editors of Time-Life Books, *The World of Winslow Homer, 1836-1910*, New York, 1966. — LLOYD GOODRICH, *Winslow Homer*, New York, 1944. — Idem, *Winslow Homer*, New York, 1959.

William Morris Hunt: HELEN M. KNOWLTON, *Art-Life of William Morris Hunt*, Boston, 1899. — MARTHA A. S. SHANNON, *Boston Days of William Morris Hunt*, Boston, 1923.

George Inness: ELLIOT DANGERFIELD, *George Inness: the Man and His Art*, New York, 1911. — GEORGE INNESS, Jr., *Life, Art and Letters of George Inness*, New York, 1917. — LEROY IRELAND, *The Works of George Inness; an Illustrated Catalogue Raisonné*, Austin (Tex.), 1965. — ELIZABETH McCAUSLAND, *George Inness, an American Landscape Painter, 1825-1894*, New York, 1946.

John Wesley Jarvis: HAROLD E. DICKSON, *John Wesley Jarvis, American Painter, 1780-1840*, New York, 1949.

Eastman Johnson: JOHN I. H. BAUR, *An American Genre Painter: Eastman Johnson, 1824-1906*, Brooklyn, 1940.

Henrietta Johnston: MARGARET SIMONS MIDDLETON, *Henrietta Johnston of Charles Town, South Carolina, America's First Pastellist*, Columbia (S.C.), 1966.

Matthew Harris Jouett: E. A. JONAS, *Matthew Harris Jouett, Kentucky Portrait Painter, 1787-1827*, Louisville (Ky.), 1938.

John La Farge: ROYAL CORTISSOZ, *John La Farge: a Memoir and a Study*, Boston and New York, 1911.

Fitz Hugh Lane: JOHN WILMERDING, *Fitz Hugh Lane, 1804-1865, American Marine Painter*, Salem (Mass.), 1964.

Edward Greene Malbone: RUEL PARDEE TOLMAN, *The Life and Works of Edward Greene Malbone, 1777-1807*, New York, 1958.

Thomas Moran: THURMAN WILKINS, *Thomas Moran: Artist of the Mountains*, Norman (Okla.), 1966.

Samuel F. B. Morse: OLIVER W. LARKIN, *Samuel F. B. Morse and American Democratic Art*, Boston and Toronto, 1954. — CARLETON MABEE, *The American Leonardo: a Life of Samuel F. B. Morse*, New York, 1943. — EDWARD LIND MORSE, ed., *Samuel F. B. Morse, His Letters and Journals*, 2 vols., Boston and New York, 1914. — SAMUEL IRENAEUS PRIME, *The Life of Samuel F. B. Morse, LL.D., Inventor of the Electro-Magnetic Recording Telegraph*, New York, 1875.

William Sidney Mount: MARY BARTLETT COWDREY and HERMAN W. WILLIAMS, Jr., *William Sidney Mount, 1807-1868: an American Painter*, New York, 1944.

John Neagle: MARGUERITE LYNCH, *John Neagle's Diary*, Art in America XXXVII, April 1949, pp. 77-99.

William Page: JOSHUA C. TAYLOR, *William Page: the American Titian*, Chicago, 1957.

Charles Willson Peale: CHARLES COLEMAN SELLERS, *Charles Willson Peale*, 2 vols., Philadelphia, 1947. — Idem, *Portraits and Miniatures by Charles Willson Peale*, American Philosophical Society Transactions, XLII, part 1, Philadelphia, 1952.

Ammi Phillips: MARY BLACK, *Ammi Phillips: Portrait Painter 1788-1865*, New York, 1968.

Matthew Pratt: WILLIAM SAWITZKY, *Matthew Pratt, 1734-1805*, New York, 1942.

Maurice Prendergast: HEDLEY HOWELL RHYS, *Maurice Prendergast, 1859-1924*, Cambridge, 1960.

John Quidor: JOHN I. H. BAUR, *John Quidor, 1801-1881*, Brooklyn, 1942. — Idem, *John Quidor, 1801-1881*, Catalogue of an exhibition at the Whitney Museum of American Art, Munson-Williams-Proctor Institute, Rochester Memorial Art Gallery and Albany Institute of History and Art, 1965-1966.

William Ranney: FRANCIS S. GRUBAR, *William Ranney, Painter of the Early West*, Washington, D.C., 1962.

Theodore Robinson: JOHN I. H. BAUR, *Theodore Robinson, 1852-1896*, Brooklyn, 1946.

Albert P. Ryder: LLOYD GOODRICH, *Albert P. Ryder*, New York, 1959.

C. B. J. Fevre de Saint-Mémin: FILLMORE NORFLEET, *Saint-Mémin in Virginia: Portraits and Biographies*, Richmond, 1942. — Idem, *The St.-Mémin Collection of Portraits: Consisting of Seven Hundred and Sixty Medallion Portraits, Principally of Distinguished Americans*, New York, 1862.

Robert Salmon: JOHN WILMERDING, *Robert Salmon, Painter of Ship and Shore*, Boston, 1968.

John Singer Sargent: EVAN CHARTERIS, *John Sargent*, New York, 1927. — WILLIAM HOWE DOWNES, *John S. Sargent: His Life and Work*, London, 1926. — DAVID McKIBBIN, *Sargent's Boston*, Boston, 1956. — CHARLES MERRILL MOUNT, *John Singer Sargent, a Biography*, New York, 1955.

Sharples Family: KATHARINE McCOOK KNOX, *The Sharples: Their Portraits of George Washington and His Contemporaries*, New Haven, 1930.

John Sloan: VAN WYCK BROOKS, *John Sloan, a Painter's Life*, New York, 1955. — BRUCE ST. JOHN, ed., *John Sloan's New York Scene*, New York, 1965.

John Smibert: HENRY WILDER FOOTE, *John Smibert*, Cambridge, 1950. — Sir DAVID EVANS, JOHN KERSLAKE, and ANDREW OLIVER, *The Notebook of John Smibert*, Boston, 1969.

Gilbert Stuart: JAMES T. FLEXNER, *Gilbert Stuart*, New York, 1955. — JOHN HILL MORGAN, *Gilbert Stuart and His Pupils*, New York, 1939. — CHARLES MERRILL MOUNT, *Gilbert Stuart: a Biography*, New York, 1964. — LAWRENCE PARK, *Gilbert Stuart, an Illustrated Descriptive List of His Works*, 4 vols., New York, 1926. — WILLIAM T. WHITLEY, *Gilbert Stuart*, Cambridge, 1932.

Thomas Sully: EDWARD BIDDLE and MANTEL FIELDING, *The Life and Works of Thomas Sully, 1783-1872*, Philadelphia, 1921. — CHARLES H. HART, ed., *A Register of Portraits Painted by Thomas Sully, 1801-1871*, Philadelphia, 1909.

Abbott H. Thayer: NELSON C. WHITE, *Abbott H. Thayer: Painter and Naturalist*, Hartford, 1951.

Jeremiah Theus: MARGARET SIMONS MIDDLETON, *Jeremiah Theus: Colonial Artist of Charles Town*, Columbia (S.C.), 1953.

John Trumbull: THEODORE SIZER, *The Works of Colonel John Trumbull: Artist of the American Revolution*, New Haven, 1967 (first ed. 1950). — JOHN TRUMBULL, *The Autobiography of Colonel John Trumbull, Patriot Artist, 1756-1843*, ed. by Theodore Sizer, New Haven, 1953.

John H. Twachtman: Eliot Clark, *John Twachtman*, New York, 1924.

John Vanderlyn: Marius Schoonmaker, *John Vanderlyn, Artist, 1775-1852*, Kingston (N.Y.), 1950.

J. Alden Weir: Dorothy Weir Young, *The Life and Letters of J. Alden Weir*, ed. with an Introduction by Lawrence W. Chisolm, New Haven, 1960.

Robert W. Weir: Irene Weir, *Robert W. Weir*, New York, 1947.

Benjamin West: Grose Evans, *Benjamin West and the Taste of His Times*, Carbondale (Ill.), 1959. — John Galt, *Life, Studies, and Works of Benjamin West*, London, 1820 (first ed. 1816).

James A. M. Whistler: Elisabeth Luther Cary, *The Works of James McNeill Whistler*, New York and London, 1913. — Elizabeth Robins Pennell and Joseph Pennell, *The Life of James McNeill Whistler*, 2 vols., Philadelphia and London, 1908 (revised ed. 1911). — Denys Sutton, *James McNeill Whistler*, London, 1966.

Worthington Whittredge: John I. H. Baur, ed., *The Autobiography of Worthington Whittredge, 1820-1910*, Brooklyn Museum Journal I, 1942, pp. 5-68.

Richard C. Woodville: *Richard Caton Woodville, an Early American Genre Painter*, Exhibition catalogue at The Corcoran Gallery of Art, Washington, D.C., April 21-June 11, 1967.

General Index

THIS VOLUME OF THE COLLECTION "PAINTING—COLOR—HISTORY"
WAS PRODUCED BY THE TECHNICAL STAFF OF ÉDITIONS D'ART
ALBERT SKIRA, FINISHED THE TENTH DAY OF JULY NINETEEN
HUNDRED AND SIXTY-NINE.

COLOR ILLUSTRATIONS PRINTED BY

COLOR STUDIOS
IMPRIMERIES RÉUNIES S.A., LAUSANNE

TEXT IN MONOFOTO BY
IMPRIMERIE HENRI STUDER S.A., GENEVA

PLATES ENGRAVED
BY GUEZELLE & RENOUARD, PARIS

PHOTOGRAPHS BY

Lee Angle, Fort Worth, Texas (page 106); Henry B. Beville, Alexandria, Va. (pages 22, 23, 26, 29, 34, 36, 40, 81, 89, 93, 97, 114, 115, 123, 124, 130); Geoffrey Clements Inc., Staten Island, N.Y. (pages 102, 120, 127); George M. Cushing, Boston, Mass. (page 24); Johnson Photographers, Inc., Clinton, Iowa (page 100); Joseph Klima, Jr., Detroit, Mich. (page 110); Rupert Roddam, Glasgow, Scotland (page 113); Malcolm Varon, New York (pages 66, 73, 85, 121); John Webb FRPS, London (page 46); the photographic services of the following museums and galleries: Boston, Mass., Museum of Fine Arts (pages 44-45, 51, 63, 75, 88, 116); Cambridge, Mass., Fogg Art Museum (pages 27, 69, 74); Cleveland, Ohio, Museum of Art (pages 67, 70, 98); Cooperstown, N.Y., New York State Historical Association (page 82); Fort Worth, Texas, Amon Carter Museum of Western Art (page 107); Hartford, Conn., Wadsworth Atheneum (page 105); Kansas City, The William Rockhill Nelson Gallery of Art (page 104); Minneapolis, Minn., The Minneapolis Society of Fine Arts (page 122); New York, The Metropolitan Museum of Art (pages 38, 83); New York, Public Library (page 54); New York, Whitney Museum of American Art (page 125); Ottawa, The National Gallery of Canada (page 41); Philadelphia, Pa., Museum of Art (pages 52, 95); Philadelphia. The Pennsylvania Academy of the Fine Arts (pages 57, 78); San Francisco, Calif., M.H. de Young Memorial Museum (page 60); St. Louis, Missouri, City Art Museum (page 30); Washington, D.C., National Gallery of Art (pages 49, 56, 87, 91, 108, 118, 128, 129); Wellington, New Zealand, National Art Gallery and Dominion Museum (page 33); Williamsburg, Va., Abby Aldrich Rockefeller Folk Art Collection (page 76); Worcester, Mass., Art Museum (pages 16, 20); and by courtesy of Art News, New York (page 72).